Kim & Stewart,
May God bless you as you
read about Jesus' love for
His bride.
Love

# Grieving The Loss Of The Church You Love

# LARRY DAVIS

# Grieving The Loss Of The Church You Love

**Library of Congress Catalog Number: 2023952664**

| | |
|---|---|
| **Name:** | Davis, Larry, Author |
| *Title:* | *Grieving the Loss of the Church You Love* |
| | Larry Davis |
| | Advantage Books, 2024 |
| **Identifiers:** | ISBN Paperback: 978159757818 |
| | ISBN eBook: 978159757979 |
| **Subjects:** | Books › Religion › Christian Life › Inspirational |

First Printing: February 2024
24 25 26 27 28 29 30    10 9 8 7 6 5 4 3 2 1

# Acknowledgements

A book like this is never written in isolation, and I would like to, at the onset, thank several people who have made this work possible. I want to thank each of the participating churches, especially **Grace Seaford Church**, for their humility in cooperating to make this a book of authentic value and not a mere philosophical work. I am grateful for all the red pen marks that **Jamie Walker** put to each draft in editing this book. It is my prayer and hope that her efforts caused her no additional grief, pun intended. I am grateful for the artistic and graphic work of **Adrian Bradshaw** for his artwork on the cover. He is a true blessing, and I count it a privilege to be a part of his diverse and gifted ministry.

Several friends who helped with research, publication, and general support (listed alphabetically): **Pastor Jon Scott Birch, Dr. Ron Cobb, Dr. Doug DeWitt, Dr. Randy Millwood, Pastor Richard Pope, Pastor Tony Skrezecz, Pastor Bill Sterling, Pastor Tom Stolle, Pastor Mark Thomas**, and my publisher **Advantage Books**.

I want to thank my family for their support and understanding for the sacrifice of time that it takes to engage in the work of ministry. My brother **Davy Davis** and mother **Margaret Davis** for their love and what I have learned from them both in life and death. My wife, **Susan Davis,** has continued to be my greatest confidant and encourager throughout this endeavor. Without her love and support, I would have given up on this work and ministry long ago.

Finally, I would like to thank my Lord and Savior, who has given us one message, one hope, and one template for grace-filled living. Lord Jesus, may you be pleased with this book, and may it aid in your mission as you continue to raise from the dead those who have the humility to follow you into the crucified life.

# Table of Contents

*Pastor Larry Davis*

# Foreword by Richard Pope

"Memento mori" from Latin roughly translates as "remember you must die." History says Roman generals would be rewarded a "triumph" in Rome to celebrate successful military campaigns. The General would sit in a magnificent chariot and be paraded through the streets of the empire's capital. The general would be adorned with praise and cheers from the crowds. These celebrations were often the highest point in the career of a general.

Yet while the general was being cheered for and celebrated, an enslaved person sat behind him in the chariot, repeating "Memento mori." The Roman Empire implemented this tradition to prevent generals from becoming too proud, hoping it would avoid military takeovers. It wasn't uncommon in Rome for a general to become so popular, so powerful, and so feared that they would attempt to take over the Empire once fought so hard to serve.

This phrase and the surrounding philosophies greatly interested me in February of 2021. Unlike my friend Larry, who revitalized a church on the verge of death, I am a church planter. In February 2021, my wife, twenty friends, and I were working to plant Canvas Church in Salisbury, MD. We were busy buying equipment, renovating our 2,000-square-foot facility in a strip mall, recruiting launch team members, and getting the word out about our new church.

The Lord was doing incredible work in our almost-launched church. People were getting saved, and our team and the energy around our launch were multiplying. For a young, naïve church planter, it was like I was in my own personal "Triumph." There was cheering, celebrations, joy, and success, but in my body – death was brewing.

A couple of months prior, I was told that my cancer had returned for the third time. In February, amidst all the glory of the growing team and new church, I was told by the doctors that the cancer had spread, and I most likely only had 3-5 years to live.

That was my "Memento mori" moment. I was 23, excited, and newly married, and everything was going right in ministry and life. However, I was brutally reminded that I, like everyone else – must die.

This news radically changed the way we planted our church. We focused on raising other pastors before our first public service. We spent a lot of time discussing sustainability plans in case I passed away before the church became self-sufficient. But we didn't just plan for my passing; we prepared for the church's death as well. We developed a plan for when the church would inevitably close its doors (Whether I was alive or not). This staunch reminder of death in a season of new life radically changed the way we do ministry. We didn't just want to plant a church; we wanted to plant a church that would have a Gospel life, and when that Gospel life ended, we would have a Gospel death.

No one was more helpful in working through how to do this than my friend Larry. Larry led a church through a process of death and now resurrection. That same church has done countless service projects, seen tons of baptisms, and recently planted a church. I learned from watching Larry and his ministry that just like for us as Christians, how we die is just as important as how we live!

One exciting revelation for me as a new church starter with a terminal illness was the Gospel isn't about avoiding death. Following Jesus is not about preserving the life we have on earth; to the contrary – it is about dying to ourselves, our pride, our flesh, and our sins and then, after that death – living for eternity with our creator. As a young pastor, I knew these truths, but they had a profoundly more significant impact on me as I wrestled with death and life and church planting and cancer.

No matter how much we love our lives or our churches, they and we must die eventually. The imperative question is, do we want death to be beautiful, restorative, and resurrection-centered? Or do we want those deaths to be horrible, destructive, and meaningless? The Bible gives us the path to have a beautiful death where Jesus is glorified, and Larry provides us with the way to allow our churches to do the same.

*Memento mori…*

# Introduction

*[23] And Jesus answered them, "The hour has come for the Son of Man to be glorified. [24] Truly, truly, I say to you, unless a grain of wheat falls into the earth and dies, it remains alone; but if it dies, it bears much fruit. [1]*

*[19] Those whom I love, I reprove and discipline, so be zealous and repent. [20] Behold, I stand at the door and knock. If anyone hears my voice and opens the door, I will come in to him and eat with him, and he with me.[2]*

At the writing of this book, over 4,000 churches close their doors annually.[3] It is a staggering statistic! Each church and community that experiences this death is left wondering if this was an avoidable death. Was there a specific treatment, process, philosophy, or strategy that could have been useful in bringing health and healing to the deceased?

Church leaders have purchased countless books to address these questions. Many are good, and I have certainly benefited from their wisdom. But in many of those books, I have found something to be missing. The authors assume that every local church should live and that death is a final blow. Those authors, whether knowingly or unknowingly, capitalize on the prescription of a treatment plan for a dying church whose promised prognosis will bring health before death comes. While there are times that treatment can bring health, most of the churches I have worked with are very sick or are in the final stages of a disease process. As a result, church leadership attempts to lead change in a church that is clinging to a false promise of life instead of embracing a graceful God honoring death. Their curative attempts lead their

---

[1] The Holy Bible: English Standard Version (Jn 12:23–24). (2016). Crossway Bibles.

[2] The Holy Bible: English Standard Version (Re 3:19–20). (2016). Crossway Bibles.

[3] http://www.churchleadership.org/apps/articles/default.asp?articleid=42346

church toward a miracle cure instead of embracing a palliative approach that will ease their church's pain. The impending death may be delayed, but generally, the result is a more excruciating and undignified death.

In 2014, I sat down with a denominational leader (Dr. Randy Millwood) who wanted to better equip me in my next endeavor to revitalize a local church. Over some Mexican cuisine, he asked me a provocative question: Does the local church have a life cycle? At first, I was at a loss for words, but within minutes the thought dawned on me that none of the local churches mentioned in the book of Revelation gather in their original form or location today. John's revelatory words recorded in chapters 2-3 are a Biblical example of what can happen to a local gathering if they become unhealthy and unrepentant.

Where there is sickness, disease is an eventual certainty. As I meditated on this further, I reminded myself that the call of a Christian is to follow a crucified life. Many of the issues within the local churches where I have led are connected to the congregants' unwillingness to surrender to the incarnational parallel of death, burial, and resurrection. With these thoughts resonating in my heart, soul, and mind, I started to formulate an answer regarding the life cycle of a local church.

If a church can diagnose disease early enough, their leadership can certainly lead them back on a course toward health and avoid a terminal illness. Tom Rainer, a well-respected scholar, has estimated that most churches in the United States fall into one of four categories[4]:

- Healthy: 10%
- Symptoms of sickness: 40%
- Very sick: 40%
- Dying: 10%

It is my professional opinion that once a church enters what Rainer calls "Very Sick" or the "Dying" phase bringing health is highly improbable. Rainer alludes to this improbability, saying "Once they move to this stage, reversal of the deterioration is

---

[4] Rainer, Thom S.. Autopsy of a Deceased Church: 12 Ways to Keep Yours Alive (Location: 695) . B&H Publishing Group. Kindle Edition.

incredibly difficult." [5] He goes on to say, "Had the members recognized the problems earlier, help is more likely to be beneficial." [6]

The reality most churches and church leaders are unwilling to face is that if disease and sickness are left undiagnosed long enough, no treatment plan will fully correct the trajectory of that local gathering. Once they are in the actively dying phase, they move into a form of denial instead of "embracing their earthly mortality in a way that brings the most glory to God." [7] If Rainer's estimates are accurate, then approximately 190,000 churches fit into these two terminal phases.

I believe that there is a natural life cycle to a local gathering and that most churches need to walk through the process of grieving a terminal illness before they can experience the resurrection that Christ has planned for His Bride. If this process is circumvented, the church will cling to church preferences, terminal ailments, and unfruitful programs and will not be able to navigate change or embrace a new post-resurrection life. The understanding of this reality is rooted in scripture, change management literature, an understanding of Christ's atonement, and the Kübler-Ross model of understanding the grief process.

At first, this reality seems like bad news, but once under closer examination, it's easy to see that they are intimately connected with the Gospel of Christ. Christ's life, death, and resurrection are integral parts of the Good News that have brought hope and resurrection to all who embrace Him as Savior. How ironic that the same philosophy of dying to self to embrace a crucified and resurrected life illudes most churches. In many ways, the schema needed to connect this truth in application parallels our faith journey. This is one of the reasons it is good news!

When a person is coming to faith, they sometimes struggle with all that they may have to give up in surrender to make Christ Lord of their life. However, post-

---

[5] Rainer, Thom S.. Autopsy of a Deceased Church: 12 Ways to Keep Yours Alive (Location: 762) . B&H Publishing Group. Kindle Edition.

[6] Rainer, Thom S.. Autopsy of a Deceased Church: 12 Ways to Keep Yours Alive (Location: 762) . B&H Publishing Group. Kindle Edition.

[7] Rainer, Thom S.. Autopsy of a Deceased Church: 12 Ways to Keep Yours Alive (Location: 798) . B&H Publishing Group. Kindle Edition.

salvation they then look back on their experience and see that what they thought they would lose was inconsequential compared to what they gained in a relationship with Jesus. The same thing is true of churches that embrace the death process and walk through the grieving process one step at a time; eventually, they arrive at a resurrection that was not of their choosing but steeped in the sovereignty and power of God. In addition to the Gospel correlation, there is an additional benefit to this way of thinking. This way of thinking is easily understood by church leadership and especially their pastors.

Most pastors and leaders within the local church have loved their people through a grief process. That means they already have all that they need to lead their church through the grieving process. There is no need to join a new coaching network, buy the latest book or idea on revitalization, or attend the latest church conference. What's needed to lead their congregants through grief is a template for how they can confidently lead their existing church through its grief.

Furthermore, the result is not a violent change process whereby the church may lose the bulk of their congregation to embrace change but a more natural process that taps into most pastor's and leadership's desire to love their church family through a difficult time of loss. Shepherding a church through its grief does not create an adversarial situation but builds on the intimacy of the pastoral relationship with the congregation.

As a pastor, my heart has a deep-seated burden to lead churches through this process so that they can embrace the change process that leads to new life. I have seen this process take place in every church I have coached and have personally led three churches through the cycle of death, burial, and resurrection which led to what we currently call revitalization. I have also seen numerous failures to lead change in a local church when this process is ignored, regardless of the gifting, education, or experience of the pastor/leadership team.

In the chapters that follow, you will be given a negative and positive example of a dying church. Then, practical wisdom that will relate to church leadership's understanding of how to lead a church through each phase of grief. Finally, practical ways to move forward post-resurrection that encourage the resurrected church to continue to walk in their new resurrected life. My hope and prayer are that the wisdom in this book will help churches to lead compassionately through the process of grief so that they can experience the new life that our Savior has promised for all who would follow Him into death, burial, and resurrection.

## NEXT STEPS

1. Reach out to a denominational leader or consultant and ask for a professional assessment of your church's health. If you do not have access to either, reach out to a trusted leader in revitalization.

2. Purchase or create a specific journal that you will use throughout this book and process.

3. Pray that the Lord would reveal to you where you are as a church: healthy, symptoms of sickness, very sick, or dying. Ask any consultant to please assess based on these categories for clarity and unity of thought. Record in your journal both your assessment and the consultant's.

4. If you do not already have a copy, order a copy of *Autopsy of a Deceased Church* by Thom Rainer.

5. Begin to pray and ask the Lord to bring to your mind people who might form your prayer team for revitalization. Keep an active list of this team, but do not ask them to join currently. You will come back to this list often in prayer to hone it to allow the Lord to place the right people on your prayer team.

6. Read and meditate on the following passages of scripture: John 12:24-26, Revelation 2:1 – 3:22, & Luke 6:12. Journal your thoughts and impressions.

# 1

# A Glorious, Grace-Filled Death

*In place of death there was light. "So that's what it is!" he suddenly exclaimed aloud. "What joy!"* [8]

*Precious in the sight of the Lord is the death of his saints.* [9]

I have been at the bedside of many people when they have taken their last breath. My experience has come from being a hospital chaplain, a pastor of a local church, and a caretaker of family who has made the transition from this life to eternity. I have come to see and understand that faith is of paramount importance for those making this transition.

Those who lack faith cling to every moment, drawing out the process of dying and struggling for every breath as they cleave to their mortality. This is not to say that if there is a fighting chance people of faith should not fight, but when the illness is truly terminal, fighting the inevitable outcome wears both the patient and the family out and robs them both of dignity. Conversely, I have also seen those who experience what I have come to understand as a "victorious death". They have such grounded faith that they know to the depth of their soul that death is a doorway to see and be with their Savior.

My Pop Pop (Grandfather) Dick taught me so much about what a victorious death can look like. Pop Pop Dick was a dedicated, lifelong Christian who had pastored a

---

[8] Tolstoy, L. (1886). *The Death of Ivan Ilych (p. 62)*. United States: Seven Treasure Publications.

[9] *The Holy Bible: English Standard Version* (Ps 116:15). (2016). Crossway Bibles.

local church for most of his life. He had lived a full life and had been married to his wife, Ginger, for more than 55 years. During his life, he was a local Christian radio station manager, the patriarch of my wife's family, and a local church planter. He had a true zeal for life and had many reasons to be in no rush to enter eternity.

When he received a diagnosis of terminal cancer in his mid-seventies, he was not concerned. He knew by faith that the Lord would deliver him from this illness or through it. Either way, he knew his God would fully deliver. As the disease process progressed, he began to lose a lot of weight, lost sight in one eye, and had many other physical failings as the cancer attacked his physical form. As this process progressed, we visited many times to cheer him up. At the conclusion of almost every visit, the tables were turned on my wife and me. We ended up walking away from our visits encouraged and built up in our faith.

On one such occasion, I remember asking, "How are you doing?". He responded by pointing heavenward and declaring, "The Lord is so good." He went on to tell us about a hospice nurse who had been sent to care for him and how he learned that she was struggling with matters of her faith. Pop Pop Dick shared the Gospel of Christ with his nurse, led her to the Lord, and began a discipleship journey with her as she continued to visit him. At no point in the dying process did I witness a loss of faith or hope. I'm sure there were difficult moments within him as he talked to the Lord about his situation or began the grieving process with his family, but he never lost hope from my perspective or those closest to him.

On his final night on earth, his wife climbed into bed with him to be close and give comfort. She remembers that he kept reaching both hands toward heaven and moving them. By this point, he had lost the ability to share with us through words, but his soul still rang out repeatedly as he gestured with his hands held heavenward. Based on previous conversations and her intuition, she imagined that he was reaching out to heaven in a gesture of excitement to see Christ face to face. I imagined he was touching the firmament of his soon-to-be heavenly home.

He passed peacefully in his bride's arms on February 6, 2006. I am convinced he was received by his Lord and Savior with the words, *"'Well done, good and faithful servant."* [10] His joy and reward were finally realized. He had graduated into the fulfillment of his faith, and I had witnessed a victorious death and my mindset had been forever changed about the process of dying.

When you compare Pop Pop Dick's death perspective to many others you see an axiom that alludes our culture and subsequently most church leaders. Pop Pop Dick was at peace because he surrendered to the eventual and certain trajectory of his death. After all, he knew that victory over death was already won by the person of Jesus. His lack of self-centeredness brought joy to others even though he died just as Christ's death brings hope, peace, love, and joy to all those who die to self to embrace a new way of living and dying.

Over time, I began to see that most people and the majority of churches do not share this perspective. They would rather live as long as possible with a terminal illness they are comfortable with instead of embracing their own eventual and providential death. Somehow, church leadership has missed the beauty of a crucified life and the resurrection that awaits those who follow their Savior's example. However, I believe some churches are ready to follow our Savior's model if leaders would just love them toward a grace-filled death.

In the spring of 2015, I stepped down from one of the largest churches on Maryland's Eastern Shore Peninsula. After finishing a two-week fast, I sensed that the Lord was leading me to revitalize a dead church somewhere on our peninsula. As I began my search, I had many offers to pastor all over the world. It would seem that when you leave a large, successful church there are many opportunities if you want a job pastoring. However, I was not merely looking for a job: I felt a deep conviction to lead a revitalization. As I prayed and meditated on this new season, God led me to two key areas of scripture previously shared in the introduction (Jn 12:24 & Rev 2-3). These biblical convictions led me to search for a church that knew it was already dead and was ready to experience resurrection.

As offers came in from many churches, I would send them a form letter or email informing them that I was not looking to just pastor a church but wanted to lead a

---

[10] *The Holy Bible: English Standard Version* (Mt 25:23). (2016). Crossway Bibles.

church through the process of death, burial, and eventual resurrection based on the aforementioned two key texts of scripture. I believed there would be many churches ready for such a glorious and grace-filled death that leads to a resurrected life. Boy, was I wrong! Churches' initial excitement to grab up a local pastor from a successful church, shifted to rejection letter after rejection letter. I began to feel that I had misheard the Holy Spirit (it does happen) and that maybe I needed to jump on one of those pastoral offers to join another large church before I lost the window of opportunity. However, in the spring of 2015, a church named Grace Baptist Church reached out to me and said that they had been in deep prayer for more than a year and that my letter resonated with what the Spirit of God had been saying to them.

Grace had been birthed in 1959 as the town of Seaford had grown around industry. Many churches were birthed in connection to the growth of a local company (DuPont), and as people of different faith movements moved into the area, they birthed churches based on the traditions they were raised within. DuPont in Seaford was a major producer of nylon. The demand for this textile drove growth for a whole community. Local churches were also connected to this industry and its expanding community. However, like many cities and communities across our nation, the demand eventually waned.

In the mid 1980's the nylon industry began its decline. Subsequently, people moved away from the area to provide for their families. Those who had already retired remained, but as work opportunities decreased, the community shrank, and a cloud descended over Seaford. It was only a matter of time before the loss of industry would impact every area of social life, including local churches. The impact was not immediate. As older saints graduated to heaven the church began a slow almost imperceptible decline.

By the fall of 2014 Grace Baptist Church had declined to a handful of faithful members, baptisms were extremely rare, outreach to the community was not a priority, and the nursery was empty. These were all symptoms that the church was very sick; church leadership was not sure what to do or how they had arrived at such a grim prognosis. In other words, they woke up at the end of a terminal diagnosis and they were grieving the loss of the church that used to be. Like most declining churches, they idolize "the past [as] hero [... and as a result] certain symptoms developed. These symptoms can become sicknesses themselves, sicknesses that lead to death". [11]

As leadership gathered, they began to look for a new pastor. To help the church in this transitional season, they were blessed with a great interim pastor. Pastor Tom Stolle encouraged the church to pray in a way that was different than their normal prayer list. To pray about God's plan for the community around them and how the church was connected to God's heart for that community. He also reminded them that he was not the man to provide that plan and that his role would be to shepherd the church in a way to prepare for its eventual resurrection. Tom told the church one Sunday from the pulpit, "If you have to choose between making Sunday's service and the Wednesday night prayer meeting, choose the prayer meeting" because that is where God is going to begin the process of bringing life to the church.

The church leaders took Tom's advice and they set aside all of their plans and all of the resumes that had been submitted. When they met as a leadership team, they spent most of their time in prayer! As they prayed, they began to move through the grief process in a healthy way. During this same year-long process, they read the book *Autopsy of a Deceased Church* by Tom Rainer. In the book, they were confronted with the reality that there were common symptoms that led to a church's death. As they took an honest look at their church they realized and admitted through prayer that they had contributed to these health issues. They were left with no way to deny the problems. As they continued to pray, they moved through the stages of grief slowly: "Denial, Anger, Bargaining, Depression, and Acceptance". [12]

Grace woke up on the other side of the grief process and not only knew their church was dead but accepted their death as God's will. To put this into practical perspective, they had died to their way of having to run and lead their church and were now ready to do whatever God asked of them so that the Lord could raise His church back to life. Because they were no longer encumbered with trying to hold

---

[11] Rainer, Thom S.. Autopsy of a Deceased Church: 12 Ways to Keep Yours Alive. (Location 793) B&H Publishing Group. Kindle Edition.

[12] Kübler-Ross, Elisabeth; Kessler, David. On Grief and Grieving: Finding the Meaning of Grief Through the Five Stages of Loss (p. 7). Scribner. Kindle Edition.

onto power or control, they were able to surrender and hear the Lord's voice saying, *"Behold, I stand at the door and knock. If anyone hears my voice and opens the door, I will come in to him and eat with him, and he with me."* [13] As they began to hear Jesus' call to resurrection, they reinitiated the process of looking at resumes from a fresh perspective.

As they began to interview candidates, they were presented with detailed plans from multiple pastors on how they would turn the church around. However, when I was interviewed, I stood out from others they interviewed because I came with no specific detailed plan. When the leaders asked why, I told them that I thought detailed plans were premature for where they were in the process of revitalization. There were precepts and phases that we could discuss, but to have a detailed plan at this phase was arrogant and lacked wisdom. How could an outsider coming in, without knowledge of the church's history, struggles, and key leaders present a plan? The plan and the strategy would involve the existing leaders continuing to strive through prayer using the Bible as their guiding tool to see a rebirth. This intrigued the church and after prayer, they decided to invite me to preach a message.

On Palm Sunday of 2015, I preached a message on the triumphal entry of Jesus into Jerusalem. Through His relationship with His followers, they would soon walk through death, burial, and resurrection. I shared that there is always hope when you focus on the mission of Jesus exclusively and Christ's call to come and pick up your cross and follow him (Matthew 16: 24-26). The church was energized and offered me the role of their pastor but I initially declined. I wanted to be sure that this church was ready to be led through change; moreover, that they had truly died and that they were not clinging to their past life. So, I came on as their interim to test these waters.

With the existing leaders, I proposed three areas of change. We would change the worship gathering, their children's program, and the polity of the church. I reasoned if we could collaborate on these three change processes, then this church had truly died to its old self and was ready to walk in a new resurrected life. We met every week as a leadership team to pray, read scripture, and then strategize how to

---

[13] *The Holy Bible: English Standard Version* (Re 3:20). (2016). Crossway Bibles.

lead through these areas. When we came to a consensus, we would gather with the remnant of the church for a Wednesday night potluck (all churches love to eat) and present our proposed changes to the church family.

Over the next three to four months, we saw Christ show up in our prayer life, in the scriptures we were led to, and in the hearts of the remnant of the church. This was not without conflict! There were some in the congregation, especially at the Wednesday night suppers, who would voice their opposition to the changes being proposed. They were usually stuck in one of the grieving phases of the process and had not progressed to where the leaders were (total acceptance). But, because of our leader's time in prayer, bible study, and oneness of direction, they either eventually embraced their new changes or backed down in their vocal opposition. I will forever be thankful and humbled by how our Lord led His people through this process.

On one such occasion, our team had prayed through what it meant to make disciples based on our Lord's command to do so in Matthew 28: 16-20. Every church has traditions and practices that develop over time that are not necessarily biblical but focus on the way things run. How people joined our fellowship in membership was one of those traditions. It was our practice to give an alter call at the close of the service and invite anyone who wanted to join our church to come forward. If they came forward with their family, a Deacon would grab a clipboard with questions on it and interview the family in the moment. They would ask the family if they were "Born Again", if they had been "Scripturally Baptized", and if they felt led by the "Spirit of God to join this church"? If the family affirmed all three questions with a "yes," then the Deacon would present the family to those gathered, and they would vote to include or exclude the family from membership.

When our leadership prayed over this process and examined it through the lens of what Jesus meant when He called the church to make disciples by "teaching them to observe all that I have commanded you"[14], we felt this process was not effective. So, we proposed that a discipleship class be written that taught our basic values for how our church practiced their faith. This new class would be offered to prospective members, and at the end, they could make an informed decision if they felt led to

---

14 The Holy Bible: English Standard Version (Mt 28:20). (2016). Crossway Bibles.

join in a covenant partnership with our local gathering. In the class we taught what it meant to be born again, what our practice and view of baptism is, how we practice the Lord's table, what our church values and believes, how to have a daily quiet time, and be a part of a group where they share and collaborate on their faith.

When we presented this on a Wednesday night a lady rose and began to confront me in a very angry tone. She was angry that this change would no longer afford her the traditional process of bringing a friend to church who could walk the aisle and then join her church. Before I could address her concerns and begin the process of shepherding her through her anger at this change, Brother Jack Maddox gripped his walker with both hands and rose to his feet.

Jack was a retired Navy Master Chief from Texas who had been teaching bible studies and Sunday school for many years at our church. Jack was on our leadership team, and he addressed the issue in a straightforward and gruff way. He said that walking an aisle is not making disciples, it's more like joining a club. He said that many who walk those aisles don't even know what it means to be born again, or what scriptural baptism is, or who we even are as a church. Furthermore, Jack said that he thought this class would be a far better way to make disciples and he was all for it. The room fell silent, and I broke the tension by simply saying, "Yeah, what Jack said." There was some light laughter, and we moved forward.

You see, no one was going to go toe to toe with Jack. Jack was a great leader, and his integrity was well respected by all the members of the church. Jack through prayer had accepted the death of what used to be, in favor of the new resurrected life that the Lord was leading the church toward. I think it was at that very moment that I knew our church was walking in a new resurrected life and that the old church had died. It was not long after that our church completed all the aforementioned proposed changes. We voted to adopt all the changes in June of 2015.

The one I thought would not go through was the change in our polity. Our congregational church would have to vote to give away its congregational power to vote on everything and instead embrace a leader-led church council. The new council was a representative form of governance, and I thought that a Baptist church would never vote away its power. Well, I was wrong again, and that day they voted unanimously to surrender control. By this time our church was growing, baptisms were happening again, and our children's ministry was growing. The attendees saw what this new resurrected life with Christ was producing and they wanted more.

Once our church adopted all the changes, I left the room so they could openly discuss my call as their pastor. I wanted them to prayerfully and cooperatively seek God to know if I was called to lead their church in the next season. I left the room and headed to my office, but I never made it to the door. Bucky Owens (our finance chair), called me back. I thought that he called me back because someone had a question that I needed to answer so they could make a better decision. But Bucky called me back because they had already voted. When juries quickly deliberate it is usually really bad or really good. Bucky informed me that the church had voted unanimously to call me as their next pastor! I was humbled and overjoyed. I had been given the honor of seeing Jesus lead His church through death, burial, and resurrection. Moreover, when He came knocking at the door they heard His voice calling them to resurrection (Rev. 2:20)! I had witnessed a Glorious, Grace-filled Death and my hope for other churches across our nation was rekindled.

## NEXT STEPS

1. Find out if any local churches in your area have been through revitalization. Reach out to their pastor or leadership team and have lunch or coffee to hear their story. Listen carefully to how the Lord brought about a victorious death for their rebirth. Make notes in a journal that you will keep with you as you walk through your own revitalization journey.

2. Read and meditate on Matthew 16:24-28. Journal your thoughts and how you sense the Lord is speaking to you about the life cycle of His local church.

3. Come back to your prayer team list and ask the Lord if the people on it are humble of heart, teachable, and if they are more in love with Christ than the building and programs of your church.

4. Take time to journal about each potential prayer team member. Come back to this daily and pray and meditate over each potential candidate.

# 2

# A Gut Wrenching, Incident Death

*Ivan Ilych's life had been most simple and most ordinary and therefore most terrible.*[15]

*Then his wife said to him, "Do you still hold fast your integrity? Curse God and die."*[16]

For many philosophy students, the reading of *The Death of Ivan Ilych* has become foundational to their understanding of wrestling with and defining the purpose of life and death. If you are unfamiliar with the book, I would suggest you read it. It is an easy and quick read, and you will be challenged like many others to draw conclusions about life and death from its narrative. In Tolstoy's fictional narrative, we are introduced to a public official who, from every worldly perspective, is happy, successful, and fulfilled. He and his family's lives are turned upside down when he contracts a terminal illness. As you walk with this man through his illness and death, you see how his and other's self-absorbed worldview makes a horrible situation worse and untenable. However, in the end, Ivan finally surrenders gracefully to death, and in doing so also alleviates the pain he has inflicted on his family. He finds, in the end, that his death could be a release for both him and his family bringing peace and comfort.

As a young student, I had no idea that this book would share parallels to the wisdom contained in the Bible or to the science of leading a change process. For the majority of Ivan's story, we see an excruciating, painful, and self-absorbed process that makes us feel pity for him and his family. If he had learned to be less self-absorbed earlier

---

[15] Tolstoy, L. (1886). *The Death of Ivan Ilych (p. 11)*. United States: Seven Treasure Publications.

[16] *The Holy Bible: English Standard Version* (Job 2:9). (2016). Crossway Bibles.

in his life or dying process, how different would his family and his experience have been? Unfortunately, this transferable truth is parallel in people and the churches that are filled with them. But there is a better way to come to death that draws wisdom from the very life and example of Christ.

I served as a chaplain for a couple of years at a local hospital that was near a beach resort area on the East Coast. One of the unfortunate aspects of serving at a beach resort is that you attend to a lot of deaths. As a result, chaplains serve families through the initial process of grief as they experience death. It was not unusual to get an emergency call to come in for a drowning or an overdose. Some of the hardest deaths were those of children who drowned, and chaplains were called to help the family so the medical staff could remain focused on the next trauma or clinical issue.

While many deaths were vacation-related, there was also a year-round local population. As a chaplain, I not only ministered to the local community but also consulted and advised the medical staff about difficult end-of-life decisions. In my tenure at the hospital, I was honored to serve as the chair of the Medical Ethics Committee. While it has been many years since Elisabeth Kübler-Ross released her seminal work on *Death and Dying,* many doctors and medical staff still struggle to best serve those with a terminal diagnosis or end-of-life care. Kübler-Ross' work "is rightly credited with giving rise to the hospice movement—and, by extension, the new specialty of hospice and palliative medicine". [17]

Unfortunately, "Physician culture epitomize[s] the never-say-die stance [... and] avoid talking about dying." [18] Many doctors are still not trained in end-of-life care. There is also the added complexity and diversity in modern culture of having doctors from other parts of the world who have not been exposed at all to end-of-life care.

---

[17] Kübler-Ross , Elisabeth. On Death and Dying: What the Dying Have to Teach Doctors, Nurses, Clergy and Their Own Families (p. 10). Scribner. Kindle Edition.

[18] Kübler-Ross , Elisabeth. On Death and Dying: What the Dying Have to Teach Doctors, Nurses, Clergy and Their Own Families (p. 10). Scribner. Kindle Edition.

Many times, they come from a culture where "Doctors informed patients of the decisions they had made and patients accepted those decisions" without question. [19]

In the summer of 2015, a woman in her late twenties came to our hospital who was fighting a battle with cancer. For the sake of discretion, many details have been altered to guard the patient and medical staff's identity. The patient was full of life and fight and was determined to win her battle. Because of her youth and personality, she connected amiably with the staff of the hospital. Our medical teams pulled around her and aided her in her battle with compassion and zeal. Over that summer I and other chaplains saw her many times.

Every visit was enjoyable and her demeanor was consistently positive. I couldn't help but notice throughout that summer that visits happened increasingly within our ICU and that the fight was taking an increasing toll on her body as well as her family. In the fall of that same year, oncologists informed her that the treatments were not working and gave her a terminal diagnosis. They gave her 6 months to a year before she would die. Understandably, this was devastating news for her and the family.

Our palliative team was informed, and our physicians, nurses, and chaplains all visited with her and her family. We provided them with the hope that a shortened life does not reduce the quality or richness of that life. While life may be shortened, there are quality-of-life practices that could be appropriated with the time left. There were palliative treatments to maintain a certain quality of life while planning to enjoy special trips and events with her family. As chaplains, we focused on her spiritual care: we helped her to connect with the hope that was available to her both in the present and beyond death. The family and patient were absorbing all of this and coming to a healthy place to be able to enjoy the time they had left. That is when one doctor stepped in and changed everything!

One of our doctors was young and had come from a different part of the world where end-of-life training was not yet valued. There, they visited the patient in the ICU and convinced them that there were experimental treatments worthy of pursuit.

---

[19] Kübler-Ross , Elisabeth. On Death and Dying: What the Dying Have to Teach Doctors, Nurses, Clergy and Their Own Families (p. 10). Scribner. Kindle Edition.

They then offered a potential hope for a cure. While the cure was statistically a long shot, the doctor reasoned that some hope is better than none. The doctor had allowed their personal connection, worldview, and lack of training in palliative medicine to influence a young woman in a difficult situation to pursue a medical science experiment that would rob her of a higher quality of life with her family with the time she had left.

Our lead chaplain, as well as our palliative medical team, was livid! The young woman's hospital visits increased over the next few months and her days were filled with treatments that took a greater and more demonstrative toll on her and her family. The family equally embraced the hope in medical science as opposed to the eternal hope promised via faith. The treatments she received prohibited travel so she and the family gave up on some of those goals in the hope they could travel after her medical cure. She and her family were consumed in following through on the medical experiment that had little possibility of bringing a cure.

Eventually, she landed back in the ICU and even when she was hours from death, she and the family were still stuck in complete denial based on what this doctor had advised. Her last hours and weeks on this earth were filled with false hope, and invasive treatments and lacked the dignity she deserved. While there are details that amplify this sad situation, out of respect for the family and teams involved I have chosen not to include them.

This young woman's death is so different from my wife's Pop Pop in the previous chapter. While not diminishing either of their lives, examining their end-of-life decisions in juxtaposition is insightful. False hope invaded the realm of real hope. The family replaced meaningful and cherished time with a science experiment that failed to produce any quality of life. One family gracefully moved through the stages of grief while the other was jarred into a reality that was thrust upon them by a well-intentioned but ill-informed doctor. Sadly, this is the same reality that penetrates the life and death of the local church.

For the sake of discretion and confidentiality, I would like to introduce you to First Church Everywhere (FCE). While I have changed the name, First Church Everywhere is a combination of over ten real churches whose terminal trajectories are typical examples of churches that represent a Gut-Wrenching, Indecent Death.

FCE, like all churches, has a birth or origin story. They began with a small core group of people who were excited to reach their community with the love of Christ. Initially, they met in homes for Bible study.

Their gathering began to grow in a local home as they studied the first church in the New Testament and prayed for the people in their group and their community. Each of the people attending the small gathering was excited about the new church and they shared with everyone within their relational circle about this new church and its love for the community. Other than the local Bible Study, their energy was poured into activities to serve the community. They gave away food, helped with social issues, and served in partnership with other civic organizations earning the right often to share the Good News about how Christ had changed their life!

Before long, their small gathering started to grow, and they launched a local Sunday worship service at a local merchant store. The owner had become a believer through the new church's outreach efforts and this new on-fire believer closed his family's store every Sunday so that his new church could use it to share the message that had changed his family's life with his community! Before long, the church outgrew his store, and several men and women gave sacrificially to purchase property to build a sanctuary three times the size of the local store.

FCE was growing rapidly and eventually, the leadership began to receive greater pressure to be more organized and deal with some of the greater business aspects of the church. They formed a committee whose purpose was to recruit people to populate other committees that other larger churches had advised them were needed to be more successful and better organized. Everything was going great, and all the numbers were up and to the right! However, some of the founding members began to sense that something was different. While the metrics looked great, the heart of the church had shifted from the original mission to reach people with the Gospel to running the day-to-day business of the church.

The church was beginning to feel more like a business than a family focused on loving their community. Over the next few years, the church slowly turned inward evidenced by shifting focus within their programs, finances, and corporate prayer life. The church's programs were more about servicing the members and not the community. Over 90% of the finances were appropriated for internal programs and maintaining the facilities. Very little was invested in the surrounding community. When the church met to pray, the prayers focused on members' aches, pains, ohs and woes! Little time was devoted to praying for the community or discerning how the Lord was moving within missional opportunities to serve the lost.

When founding and mature members raised their concerns about the trajectory of the church turning more inward, they were reminded that the new leadership of the church now "prefer to see themselves as a hospital rather than an army" to advance the Kingdom. [20] It was further explained that if they did not keep the current attenders connected and happy funding would shrink and soon the church would not have money even for outreach.

Baptisms became less frequent as time went on, but the church remained about the same size until a few things transpired. First, almost unperceivably, attrition happened as church attenders aged and graduated to heaven (translation = they died). Because a few graduated per year, you did not notice the impact on the gathering's size immediately. Another gradual issue was that children who grew up in the church did not stay. Many moved away for school or jobs, and the ones who did stay did not feel that the church was relevant to their lives or the season they were in. They saw their childhood church as something more for the parents than for them.

Then the largest industry in the area went under. The impact on the whole community was devastating! People who were able to retire did and they stayed in the town, but those who were at the peak of their careers moved their families to other places in the country where they could continue to advance in their career and provide for their family. The industry's collapse had ripple effects in other areas of the community. Grocery stores, gas stations, restaurants, and other support businesses also took a big, significant hit. The church did not add new members and over the next few decades, the church dwindled to less than 30 attenders.

Aging leadership began to realize that they were on a trajectory for the church to not survive. They sought consultants and each consultant prescribed changes, but at this point, the church could not attract a new pastor with the skills to lead

[20] Michael Green. Evangelism in the Early Church (Kindle Locations 117-118). Kindle Edition.

complicated changes. When they reached out to recent seminary graduates, they faced several obstacles to attracting them to their church.

Seminary students had accumulated a lot of school debt based on their pursuit of a graduate degree that was typically more than 100 hours. Most fully trained seminary students could not entertain a bi-vocational situation because their educational training was only religious. Additionally, many students had grown excited to plant a church, not work in the realm of revitalization. They had heard from several experts that "it is easier to give birth than raise the dead". If any candidates, seminary-trained or not, showed interest they faced a congregation who was resistant to any suggestions of change or innovation.

One local candidate being interviewed suggested the church sync up the adult curriculum with the children's curriculum to better create spiritual conversations within attending families. A previous pastor who was still attending the church told the congregation that it was an idea that came from a more liberal, famous pastor and the church dismissed the idea. The candidate, seeing that the church was not willing to bargain over a small change, gave up and decided to plant instead in an adjacent community. Additionally, their reserve fund had been spent maintaining their building and property.

FCE eventually got to a place where they knew that things were critical. They tried all kinds of gimmicks to save the church. They did fundraisers and movie nights in the local park and put out local advertisements to try and let people know about their church. They updated their church sign and even brought in guest preachers that they thought would be attractional. But all the bargaining only led to greater frustration. The church was willing to blame everyone except themselves for the decline in members/attendees.

When their efforts did bring a visiting family, the family had a poor first-time visit. The church's service was completely geared to the faithful few and little consideration was given to guests. The visiting family was usually asked to stand and identify themselves, which singled them out and made them feel uncomfortable. There was no programming for the children, so the family did not feel the church was family friendly.

Because there was inconsistency in the pulpit, the Gospel was not presented weekly. The message was typically more about certain theological truths that were of interest to the gathered remnant or the guest preacher. Worst of all, the church had become so inward-focused that no member even greeted visiting families or spent time trying to get to know them. Because of this, no family returned, and the church's efforts were not bearing any fruit.

A denominational leader brought in a consultant to help advise the church. The consultant suggested that they read *Autopsy of a Deceased Church* by Tom Rainer and prayerfully consider if they, like many other churches in decline, had committed some of the same errors that led to other church's death. The church leadership read the book and was deeply offended by the common issues that the book brought up. They did not have the humility to see that they were like many other churches and that they had indeed committed some of the same mistakes that typically lead to a church's death.

When they gathered in business meetings, they would say that the world had changed too much, that the nation was no longer Christian and this was why no one would attend their church. They blamed current and former pastors for their inadequacy to lead. Eventually, they stopped pointing the finger and settled into the reality that their church was dying. As this happened, a deep depression settled over the church.

As the depression settled in over a few years, there was an eventual apathy or resignation that the church would die and there was nothing that could change that fact. The older congregants that had stayed had run out of energy and hope. Because bills still needed to be paid to maintain the building and property the church leadership decided to sell all assets. An insurance company bought the property at a very low market rate, leaving the church with just enough money to pay off its debt and bring bills up to date. It was a very sad situation and when FCE closed its doors, the few existing members transferred to other churches that fit their consumeristic preferences.

In the end, FCE lost its way and was unwilling to embrace change when initial signs of sickness were brought up by founding members. They slowly shifted from a Gospel-centered church to a church that provided religious commodities to religious consumers. When they were confronted with the issues that had led to their terminal trajectory, they ignored them by denying them or rationalizing them away. Even their prayer life pulled inward, and they lost their heart for the marginalized, hurting, and lost within their community.

While FCE could have been saved and brought to health when the issues of unhealth were raised, it was their ignoring and rationalizing of the issues that brought them on an unrecoverable trajectory. Even more tragic was their inability to see the hope that lay beyond their church's death. The final members just found new churches that met their needs; they were not willing to restart, replant, or turn over their church to another church to begin a new work reaching and discipling their community. While all churches have a life cycle, not all need to die physically or tragically: they can embrace a more graceful death when they understand that change, like death, is a certainty that can be navigated via the wisdom contained in the grief process.

## NEXT STEPS

1. Consider the difference between a Victorious Death vs a Gut-Wrenching one. Do you have a sense of which one your current church is headed? Write down your impression in your journal and have an honest conversation with the Lord about it.

2. Allow the Lord to bring to your mind a church or a person that has experienced either type of death: Victorious or Gut-Wrenching. Discuss the dichotomy with a colleague or trusted leader. Journal your thoughts.

3. Come back to your list for your prayer team. Ask the Holy Spirit which type of death each person might embrace. If you feel led, explain the two types of deaths, and ask a potential team member their thoughts.

4. Based on your prayer life, conversations, and the Holy Spirit's leading narrow your prayer team to 5-7 people. Record in your journal and invite each person to your first prayer meeting.

5. Set a weekly time to meet for 60-90 minutes for prayer and discussion and ask each person if they would like to be on your prayer team for the revitalization of your church.

6. At your first meeting explain that you have been reading this book and that you would like them to pray with you, study with you, and help work through the process of revitalization as a church.

7. Let them know that in addition to the weekly prayer meeting, they will be putting in time reading and praying daily for the church. Graciously allow those to leave who can't make the commitment. Later thank God for the team He has provided you to walk through this revitalization!

8. Ask your new team to purchase a copy of this book as well as Autopsy of a Deceased Church.

9. Once they receive a copy of this book, let them catch up to this chapter. They should be able to do it within a week of getting the book.

10. At your weekly prayer meeting take time to discuss each chapter and allow it to impact your time in prayer together.

11. Once your team is caught up, move to the next chapter.

# 3

# The Change Process & Grief

*"Transformation is a process, not an event".* [21]

*"For everything there is a season, and a time for every matter under heaven".* [22]

John Kotter is a leading authority on Change Management. His eight-step process has been the starting point of many theories and change processes. When I attended a church seminar on revitalization, we were told to read everything we could on Change Management since that is what you are addressing within a dying or unhealthy church. Therefore, it is surprising that businesses and churches have studied Kotter's publications to better understand how they might lead or create a change, but few have slowed down enough to consider the why behind change management theory.

I had a difficult time in my early education (elementary - middle school). If you were to ask my teachers why, I'm sure you would get a plethora of humorous answers. It was not uncommon for my report card to have comments like: "Can't sit still, Won't stop talking, Constantly Figits". These were all great signs of what we label ADHD. But I can tell you at the root of my behavior was boredom with the traditional education system.

As I have reflected, I have come to understand that other than being hyperactive, I had to know the "why" before I could understand the "how" or "what". Every time

---

[21] Harvard Business Review. HBR's 10 Must Reads on Change Management (Location: 53). Perseus Books Group. Kindle Edition.

[22] *The Holy Bible: English Standard Version* (Ec 3:1). (2016). Crossway Bibles.

a teacher would explain something, I was the kid who would raise his hand and ask "WHY?" I see this in many young children, and when they ask this of a teacher/instructor the instructor can get a little frustrated. They are not generally frustrated with the child but are frustrated that they were never provided with the "why" and consequently are not able to provide the answer. When I see that situation today, I laugh inside and seek out that "WHY-SEEKER" and encourage them to never stop asking to know the "why".

Many people grow out of this way of thinking, but for some reason I never did. I was eventually able to find teachers who embraced the "why" and had a greater understanding of the root of the subject material. I have always connected with these types of thinkers. I was exuberant when I finally watched Simon Sinek's TED Talk on *Start with Why*. When you know the "WHY" you have a better starting point for understanding and you can better question, engage, and contextualize with the wisdom of any author.

When you dig into John Kotter's Change Management process, you discover that change management processes are derived and rooted in the grieving process that Kübler-Ross wrote about in *On Death and Dying*. Notice that Kübler-Ross' research was about loss and how someone processes loss. Physical Death is one aspect, but you can grieve many different types of losses: You can grieve the loss of a relationship (divorce), the loss of a job, the loss of a child moving out (empty nester), or any other dimension of life where you have a sense of forfeiture.

Many businesses and organizations have already made this discovery and have started to think about leading change as a process of leading their people through the process of grief. One of the best and most concise books I have read is *HBR's 10 Must Reads on Change Management*. In the book, you can see visible signs of the resistance to accept change as people grieve.

> Leading major organizational change often involves radically reconfiguring a complex network of people, tasks, and institutions that have achieved a kind of modus vivendi, no matter how dysfunctional it appears to you. When the status quo is upset, people feel a sense of profound loss and dashed expectations. They may go through a period of feeling

incompetent or disloyal. It's no wonder they resist the change or try to eliminate its visible agent. [23]

You can also see these signs easily in a church that is very sick or dying. I have seen them manifest in some very interesting ways. Churches deny often that there is a core issue altogether that is leading to their unhealth by saying that they are just in a season of decline and that they will soon rebound. I had a church once tell me that the reason for their decline was that they did not have enough letters for their church sign; therefore, people did not want to attend because they were ill-informed (bargaining). One of the most common expressions of anger is to blame a pastor or a church leader for the decline. I think this is why you see a high rate of turnover in those churches. There are hundreds of examples that demonstrate expressed grief, and the need to understand its connection to change management is paramount.

Not long ago, I was biking with a pastoral colleague who was grieving being let go by his former church. He was deeply wounded because he loved his former church. What he failed to see is that he tried to lead the church through change while they were still in the early stages of their grief. Consequently, they were not ready and as a result, a group of influential leaders turned their anger toward him resulting in his dismissal. If you or I try to force change on an organization that has not been properly prepared for change, then we will also suffer a similar fate. This is why understanding the WHY of Change Management is connected to the grief process.

Once you know that this is the WHY that Change Management is built on, you begin to discover all kinds of new realities that are connected to the grieving process of a church or organization. You also are encouraged, because churches and their leadership are uniquely equipped to help people through the grieving process and generally have experience doing just that. Another powerful asset to connecting grief to managing change is that it taps into the emotive resistance to change. When you give some thought to the reason why most churches resist change, it is not anchored in reason but emotion.

---

[23] Harvard Business Review. HBR's 10 Must Reads on Change Management

(Location: 1659). Perseus Books Group. Kindle Edition.

I have a background in engineering so when I first arrived at the church, I knew I could use my gifts around technology to help the church. I also had a background in worship and the arts, and so when I began to look at the technical infrastructure of the church, I saw some quick areas that needed to be changed. When you are looking to build momentum in an organization that has been static for a long time it is helpful to look for low-hanging fruit. Many times, low-hanging fruit can be identified by looking for strengths in gifting, and in changes that most people will not think are earth-moving yet can benefit the church or organization. One of my first changes was to remove the computer that was being used for worship and update it with something that would be more efficient, current, and easier to use. However, I did not expect that I would get resistance from the former choir director.

The former choir director was a former engineer as well (mechanical engineer) and had gone to Virginia Tech for his training. He is a smart man who also has many gifts and talents in worship/music ministry; additionally, he plays a mean saxophone. Even though he was in his eighties at the time, I was pleasantly surprised to see that he was very tech-savvy. So, I was shocked when he presented a visceral objective to update the sanctuary computer at a worship meeting.

I met with him and the worship team and explained the situation. The computer was more than 10 years old, the operating system was no longer being supported, the graphic interfaces were insufficient for the multi-display upgrade that was coming, the computer's speed and capabilities could not run any of the modern software that was needed, and its audio interfaces were unable to be easily used with the new audio upgrades. Any engineer worth his salt would understand from reason and experience that this older tech needed to go! It was obvious that logic or reason were not driving his objection. When I met with him later in private, I learned that he had donated that computer in memory of his now-deceased wife. Talk about a change process connected to grief!

Once I learned of his emotional attachment to this computer and its connection to his grief, I asked him if it would be okay to repurpose the computer at the welcome desk for attendees to use to look up things on the internet, purchase bible study materials, and interface with our new online database. The computer would be able to be used in that way and it would allow us to move forward with the right computer in the sanctuary for our projection and multimedia needs. He excitedly agreed. It was not reason that won the day but tapping into the emotive aspect of helping him to process his grief.

This is why it is important to understand that every change is connected to the loss of something for someone in your church or organization. To this day, I maintain a wonderful relationship with this former choir director and worship leader. I had earned his trust by showing care for his emotions and his grief. When I brought the next change to his worship team he was even more supportive and became one of my biggest advocates in helping me lead through change: all because I had learned that resistance to change is not usually about a logic problem but is connected to an emotion that must be processed. He is now in assisted living, and I miss him and cherish the few times I get to visit him with one of our deacons. He taught me a lot about love, humility, and how to build relationships through worship in our church.

Whether you are a leader, congregant, or the current pastor you should be encouraged by the connection of grief to leading change. Why is that? Because it offers you a compassionate opportunity to love your church through the process. This relational approach to leading change leaves fewer wounded attenders and leaders in the wake of the change process that the Lord is calling a church to walk through. While I could write a whole book on the processes of leading change, that is not the purpose of this chapter or book. I simply want to introduce you to the need to recognize the power of emotion connected to grief and how that emotion needs to be addressed carefully and methodically before and while you lead change.

One of John Kotter's warnings as to why many change processes fail has to do with "Not Creating a Powerful Enough Guiding Coalition". [24] Organizations "that fail in phase two usually underestimate the difficulties of producing change and thus the importance of a powerful guiding coalition." [25] What I am presenting here, is that

---

[24] Harvard Business Review. HBR's 10 Must Reads on Change Management (Location: 105). Perseus Books Group. Kindle Edition.

[25] Harvard Business Review. HBR's 10 Must Reads on Change Management (Location: 125). Perseus Books Group. Kindle Edition.

the way we build that guiding coalition is by shepherding a church through their grief.

They must grieve the church that was before they can embrace the church that will be resurrected. If we rush this process or try to ram through a change with a dying church, we will only create more hurt and harm. Instead, humbly recognize your role as the leader to love your people through grieving the loss that is logically before them and when they finally arrive at acceptance, then you are ready to present a new vision for the church that God is resurrecting.

When I arrived at my current church, Grace Seaford, the whole of the church had already grieved what was and was ready for change. But there were a few laggards who were still holding on to the church that was and had not caught up to the rest of the church who had accepted the new trajectory of our church. Within a long-standing Sunday School were a few ladies who were still struggling to embrace the new direction our church headed.

Their struggle was brought to a boiling point when I needed to move their Sunday School to accommodate our growing children's program. There were a few ladies in the Sunday school that the deacons and leaders were afraid to approach about changing their location. They occupied a specific room down the old Sunday school wing. We needed to change the old Sunday school wing into an area for our children's ministry, that would be safe and isolated and allow parents a secure check-in area for their children. We had more Sunday school spaces at the front of the church that were available. However, I was soon informed by our leaders and Deacons that they believed this group of ladies was not willing to surrender their Sunday school room.

I asked our deacons, and our leaders why this was so. No one can answer the question. And no existing leader was willing to confront this group of women. All the old leaders assumed that these ladies were unwilling to accept this inconvenient change. When I asked, "Why are you all afraid to confront these women about changing their Sunday school space?", they said unequivocally there were specific individuals within the group who had been vocal about their opposition to previous changes based on the new trajectory of the church.

With a little further research, I learned there was a history here. And that there were a couple of women in the group who had been vocally opposed to any change in their church. Especially change that may upset their routine or class. So, I let our leadership know that I would deal with this problem when I finished worship rehearsal the following Sunday. I would go and engage these women. By the end of our confrontation, they would be moving their Sunday school class.

The time came for my confrontation that Sunday, and I headed straight for their Sunday school class. I was met in the hallway by a wonderful, sweet woman that I would later learn is one of the greatest leaders I've ever known: Mrs. Julia Mills! She informed me that she had just come from that Sunday school class, that she had spoken to the ladies that were there, and that they would be moving the following week. Furthermore, she would be helping them in their transition to their new Sunday school class in front of the church. Mrs. Julia was the leader of that Sunday School class and one of the most genuine Christians I have ever met.

Later, I learned that Mrs. Julia had shared her love for the changed lives that were emerging in our church. She loved seeing the children's ministry being filled again, baptisms of new believers, and seeing young families attending again. She was concerned that these women, who were reluctant to change, might miss the bigger picture of what God was doing in their church. She made a bold and courageous move as a leader and confronted members of her Sunday School who were having a hard time with the proposed change. In other words, SHE ADDRESSED THE WHY!

I was so impressed with her, that I immediately put her on our leadership team. She continues to impress me not only with her leadership but her dedicated prayer life over our church and for me as her pastor! I watched this amazing woman also take time away from her leadership responsibilities to care for her husband who had Parkinson's and eventually died of a stroke. She showed the same determinism in his care, her marriage, and in her preservation of his dignity.

Mrs. Julia was part of a guiding coalition that caught God's vision for change based on our team building healthy relationships about the change process. Mr. Jack, and countless other older saints, also were instrumental in seeing change happen because we took the time to build a trusting relationship with them. We learned from one another and supported each other through the needed changes that our church navigated out of a post resurrected life.

Please note that the reality shared in this chapter applies to a church that is actively dying and that a different approach to leading change is needed for a church that is healthy or has the initial symptoms of sickness. If your church or organization is healthy or showing initial signs of sickness and you know that leading change is necessary to lead out of a slump to a new growth cycle, please seek a consultant who can help guide you through leading a change process. You may also reach out to me for a statewide training that I have done for leading a 4-step change process. I will briefly cover that process later in the chapter titled "Living the Resurrected Life".

## NEXT STEPS

1. When you meet with your prayer team, ask if any of the leaders have experience with leading a change process. Ask if they know of anyone in the church who may have experience with Change Management. Write those names down in your journal for future reference and potentially to be added to the team that will implement change.

2. Pray that the Lord would begin to show WHY the church needs to be led through change. In what way is He calling your church to change for the benefit of the community or the Kingdom of God?

3. Watch Simon Sinek's *Start with Why* with your prayer team. Begin to consider WHY your church exists. Consider Simon's "Golden Circle" and how it impacts your communication methods as a church.

4. Ask your prayer team to begin to search God's heart for WHY your church needs change, HOW that change will impact your community and Christ's Kingdom, and WHAT challenges may impede change from the congregation.

*Pastor Larry Davis*

# 4

# Denial

*Martha said to Jesus, "Lord, if you had been here, my brother would not have died.[26]*

*And you may have been like I was with my father. It's not happening. Denial. But now it's time to let go. Holding on will do no one any good. A dying church is of little benefit to the Kingdom . . . unless it dies well.[27]*

Denial gets a bad rap both in our society as a whole and especially in grief. It is easy to look at this stage of grief as a weakness, especially if the phase is prolonged. But Denial has a purpose along the continuum of grief, and it is not the polar opposite of acceptance. If your church is primarily dealing with denial, it would be a mistake to think that you can shock or force them to move forward through will or force. The result of such an approach will more than likely lead to more pain both for the church and the leadership. To first understand how to lead your church through this phase let's spend some time trying to best understand denial within the substrate of grief.

According to Kübler-Ross' research, "Denial functions as a buffer after unexpected shocking news, allow[ing] the patient to collect himself and, with time, mobilize other, less radical defenses."[28] The reality is that some truths are difficult to stomach and if forced upon us too soon, or before we are ready to process them, they only

---

[26] *The Holy Bible: English Standard Version* (Jn 11:21). (2016). Crossway Bibles.

[27] Rainer, Thom S.. Autopsy of a Deceased Church: 12 Ways to Keep Yours Alive (Location: 817) . B&H Publishing Group. Kindle Edition.

[28] Kübler-Ross , Elisabeth. On Death and Dying: What the Dying Have to Teach Doctors, Nurses, Clergy and Their Own Families (p. 52). Scribner. Kindle Edition.

create greater damage. Therefore, we need to many times create or manufacture a way to slow down the impact of grief so that our emotions can catch up. Denial for many is that mechanism. "Denial helps us to pace our feelings of grief. There is a grace in denial. It is nature's way of letting in only as much as we can handle." [29] When viewed from this place, denial requires a tactful hand and a discerning heart. It requires an equal measure of grace and truth at appropriate, discerned moments that are brought to the forefront by a tactful team or individual who has earned the trust of those in denial. The intensity and speed by which someone works through denial are proportional to the harshness and relational proximity of the one delivering the bad news.

In 2010, at the age of 47, my older brother was diagnosed with a rare form of lung cancer. Because I was in a ministry role, my church afforded me the opportunity to stay with my brother throughout his hospitalization. I was not expecting to hear a terminal diagnosis, but my suspicions grew as days turned into weeks. The local hospital was befuddled, and after a couple of weeks transferred my brother to Johns Hopkins in Baltimore, MD. Because my family was all working, I accompanied him on his exploration to discover what was attacking his well-being.

My brother was almost ten years my senior and stood beside me and my mother when my father abandoned us (I was fourteen at the time). My brother was only twenty-four and I did not fully comprehend his sacrifice to stay behind to help my mom raise me. He was an amazing, gifted man and we shared a very special relationship that went beyond brotherhood. He was my mentor, music teacher, confidant, and even surrogate father. I knew he was very sick, but when he was transferred to one of the best research hospitals in the world, I was certain everything was going to be okay. I had also prayed with him and for him and could conceive of no justice in his sickness ending in death.

Once at Hopkins, they performed a biopsy on his lymph nodes to gain a better perspective to diagnose him. After the surgical biopsy, he was placed in the ICU and remained on a ventilator as he recovered. My sister came up to give me a break, since

---

[29] Kübler-Ross, Elisabeth; Kessler, David. On Grief and Grieving: Finding the Meaning of Grief Through the Five Stages of Loss (p. 10). Scribner. Kindle Edition.

we live two hours away, and I took that opportunity to rush home and see my wife and children. When she called the next day, she shattered my world with the malignant findings and urged me to rush back to the hospital.

When I arrived at the ICU the doctor informed me that my brother could not be weaned off the ventilator because his lungs were so damaged from the cancer that his $CO_2$ rose to lethal levels every time. When we met with the oncologist, she informed me that the only treatment for the type of cancer my brother had was chemotherapy. The problem was the prescribed treatment would kill him.

When I asked the ICU doctor what we should do he said, "If it was my brother, I would take him off the ventilator and let him die peacefully". I asked how much time we had, and he told us "Hours once he was removed from the ventilator". Both doctors were sharing the truth with me, but I was not ready to process what they were saying. I called a friend of mine who is a doctor and explained the situation, and he confirmed what I was being told. My sister also brought her many years of nursing to bear on the situation and helped me process what was being shared. In the end, it was not the professional or the expert that swayed me, but my friends and family who brought me through my denial.

Hopkins had a hospice floor, and we took my brother off the ventilator and moved him there. He was released to be off the ventilator, and we drew close as an extended family to be with him. By then his fiancé, my wife and several cousins and relatives had arrived. One of my brother's greatest regrets was not being married so I performed a religious wedding (not legal) for him and his fiancé hours before he passed. He died happy, secure in his faith and surrounded by his family. I held his hand until his heart took its last beat and, while the memory is surreal, I was still in denial that what was taking place was real! What brought me through my denial were those closest to me, and the truth that Christ's Gospel had saved him: it provided me with the hope and assurance that I would see him again. Your church needs the same truth and relational proximity to process their death in anticipation of a future resurrection. That is how we lead those we love through denial.

How does a leadership team or pastor earn the trust of a church in denial? They do so by sharing in equal measure the incarnate qualities of grace and truth. One of the greatest ways to share truth is through the pulpit or teaching. The Word of God is power and "is living and active, sharper than any two-edged sword, piercing to the division of soul and of spirit, of joints and of marrow, and discerning the thoughts and intentions of the heart." [30] One of the keys to addressing denial with the truth of God's Word is to exegete the people before you exegete the text. What I mean is, in your prayer life with your team, allow the Holy Spirit to reveal to you what specific areas the church is in denial about. Then, develop a message or series connected to that specific issue. What does this look like? As an example, when I arrived at my current church, I discerned two things very quickly.

One, the church did not fully comprehend how hard it is to revitalize a church. Two, they somehow had developed a mindset that I as the pastor would magically recruit all these young people who would show up and do all the work that the existing leaders were too worn out to do. In both realities, there was a denial to deal with the truth that you are never too old to do ministry and that the enemy would come powerfully against what God was calling us to do. So, for one of my first sermon series I preached through the issue of spiritual warfare.

We entitled the series "ALL OUT WAR" and walked through the Apostle Paul's wisdom about putting on the full armor of God in Ephesians 6. By the end of the series, we had confronted how the enemy would come against us as we pressed forward with the death, burial, and resurrection of our church. The people of the church were personally prepared and understood that this would be difficult and that no one was going to swoop in and solve everything with a magical fix.

Additionally, they began to frame expectations correctly of themselves and their pastor. Next, we walked through the Book of Nehemiah and the church saw that everyone had a role to play in the renewal of God's church. You're not done if you continue to draw breath. The Nehemiah series brought excitement and reminded the remnant of their integral part in the next season of renewal. In each of these areas, I was able to address the truth and dispel their poor understanding as well as years of poor discipleship within the church. As stated earlier, in addition to the truth you need to address the emotive issue within denial.

---

[30] *The Holy Bible: English Standard Version* (Heb 4:12). (2016). Crossway Bibles.

We addressed the emotional aspect of denial by launching Wednesday night cover dish dinners with a time of unscripted teaching. Each time a person in the congregation brought up an emotional response to a change, a leader was chosen to follow up and relationally talk through the objection with them. The key here is based on the depth of the relationship that has been earned. I told our core team early on that the congregation would not come to me with their complaints and objections to proposed changes. They would instead come to established and trusted leaders they had built relations with. My role was to equip existing leaders with the truth of what a New Testament church is called to be, and then encourage them to lead their friends through their denial. You see this parallel with patients who struggle with denial.

The reality is that "patients can be quite selective in choosing different people among family members or staff with whom they discuss matters of their illness or impending death while pretending to get well with those who cannot tolerate the thought of their demise." [31] This duality is common to our human condition, but when you share truth from a place of relationship you can bring integrity to the individual as well as the church. While Denial may not just be a river in Egypt, it can cut deeply into the heart of the Land of Change. It has been my experience in the larger gathering that more than 80% of the church will work through denial when you employ the aforementioned process and that less than 20% will fall into what The Diffusion of Innovations theory calls "Laggards". [32] But what do you do with those Laggards?

The reality is that your patience will eventually arrive at a precipice, and this will be when discernment and prayer will chart the pathway forward. You will reach a place where you know a group or individual is now in denial because of disobedience or a competing, unbiblical agenda. When you arrive at this place you will need to take a stronger position and support the majority of the church who have moved

---

[31] Kübler-Ross, Elisabeth. On Death and Dying: What the Dying Have to Teach Doctors, Nurses, Clergy and Their Own Families (p. 55). Scribner. Kindle Edition.

[32] Rogers, E. M. (1962). *Diffusion of Innovations* (1st ed., pp. 171). Collier-Macmillan, Ltd.

past this phase. If you do not, you will allow the Enemy to hold captive the church for the disobedience of those who are impeding the Kingdom.

Even Kübler-Ross saw there is a moment where you can no longer go along with untruth regarding a person's difficulty in accepting death. With one patient their denial resulted in personal harm to their body and their family. "This was intolerable and we told her so. This was part of reality that we could not deny with her." [33] Eventually, this patient had to be confronted because of how it was impacting their care. You too will face this situation and prayer and discernment will be your greatest tools to understand how to respond properly.

You will find that denial could be connected to preference, a power play, or ignorance of what the New Testament Church is called to be and do. Additionally, you will find that all the right people are at your church to deal with the situation. Eventually, all those stuck in denial will move on or forward in some measure. While I lost very few established members when bringing change, the few who moved on were in complete denial regarding problems within the church. In the end, I pointed them to a church that met their needs while allowing us to move forward. This is a healthy response for both them and the church and you will be called to lead through these situations.

I can say that one area where the Kübler-Ross model falls completely short when addressing denial is on the faith side of the paradigm. In her research she expressed that a dying patient "may share some important fantasies about death itself or life after death (a denial in itself), only to change the topic after a few minutes, almost contradicting what he said earlier." [34] It is the hope of the resurrection (life after death) that is the truth that assures us to move through denial because of the certainty that death cannot win in the life of the true believer.

This is not another form of denial, but a certainty that enables the true believer to face their death, as well as the local church's corporate death with the hope of

---

[33] Kübler-Ross , Elisabeth. On Death and Dying: What the Dying Have to Teach Doctors, Nurses, Clergy and Their Own Families (p. 58). Scribner. Kindle Edition.

[34] Kübler-Ross , Elisabeth. On Death and Dying: What the Dying Have to Teach Doctors, Nurses, Clergy and Their Own Families (p. 54). Scribner. Kindle Edition.

Grieving the Loss of the Church You Love

resurrection! While your church may die to who it used to be, there is a glorious resurrection waiting for those who don't get stuck in denial or the grieving process. However, don't be surprised if emotions run high and those emotions target you.

Just remember that Christ took on the hatred of a culture that was clinging to power, control, and tradition. Furthermore, He was willing to take it on for the benefit and redemption of those not yet born. If we can embrace Christ's heart and mission incarnationally, then we too might see the Kingdom grow through our own unjust crucifixion. Would that not be one of the greatest honors we could ever share with our Savior?

## NEXT STEPS

1. Ask your prayer team to spend an extended time in prayer asking the Lord to reveal to you where people are in Denial about your church (be specific).

2. Share how the Lord is revealing denial, and how you have personally experienced it, and avoid the temptation to villainize or gossip about church attendees who have shared about their denial while still being specific. Remind the team that conversations within the prayer team are confidential.

3. Work with your prayer team, and teaching team if you have one, to construct a sermon series that will address various aspects of denial. If you have a difficult time with this email me at pastor@graceseaford.org and I will send you the one that we used.

4. Begin meeting consistently with the congregation (not on Sunday) and create a safe place for them to express their concerns.

5. When concerns are brought up address them in the public meeting, but also have specific leaders (who have a relationship with the one raising the concern) follow up to help them process how they are feeling and why change is so important if the church is to experience a new life.

# 5

# Anger

*²⁰ for the anger of man does not produce the righteousness of God.* [35]

*Anger choked him and he was agonizingly, unbearably miserable. "It is impossible that all men have been doomed to suffer this awful horror!"* [36]

Once reality penetrates denial, strong emotions can flow through people. "When the first stage of denial cannot be maintained any longer, it is replaced by feelings of anger, rage, envy, and resentment. The logical next question becomes: "Why me?" [37] While anger is not always the primary emotion, it is common among people who are dealing with grief. A dying church and the people who are in it will express their anger in unique ways. They might play the blame game, become cold or withdrawn to leadership, or even instigate a fight. They may even build a coalition sharing their view and then confront those leading or proposing change. Ultimately, if emotions run high, and for a prolonged period, they will even try and remove existing leadership to maintain power or the status quo. This is why guiding them to express and manage their anger is a critical phase if you are to move forward.

If you have never experienced grief in a personal way, you may not be aware that "Anger does not have to be logical or valid." [38] "In contrast to the stage of denial,

---

[35] *The Holy Bible: English Standard Version* (Jas 1:20). (2016). Crossway Bibles.

[36] Tolstoy, L. (1886). *The Death of Ivan Ilych (p. 35)*. United States: Seven Treasure Publications.

[37] Kübler-Ross , Elisabeth. On Death and Dying: What the Dying Have to Teach Doctors, Nurses, Clergy and Their Own Families (p. 63). Scribner. Kindle Edition.

[38] Kübler-Ross, Elisabeth; Kessler, David. On Grief and Grieving: Finding the Meaning of Grief Through the Five Stages of Loss (p. 11). Scribner. Kindle Edition.

this stage of anger is very difficult to cope with from the point of view of [... those closest to the church] and [the] staff. The reason for this is the fact that this anger is displaced in all directions and projected onto the environment at times almost at random." [39] While this is truer of vented anger or rage, at other times there is less randomness and even a fixation on specific people or situations.

When I arrived at my church, I surveyed my community door to door to gain greater insight. One, would they share with me ways to reach them based on social problems and what did they understand about our church historically? I quickly learned that the community was looking for a church that was willing to engage within the community and did not create situations where the community had to come to the church.

They were communicating that they wanted the church to get out of its four walls and be a part of the community. I also learned that there was a perception of our church historically as the all-white, rich DuPont (largest industry) church. When I learned this perceived reality, I thought it would be a good idea to rebrand our church. We were birthed in the late 1950's as Grace Baptist Church. So, working with the leadership team, we changed the name of the church to Grace Seaford Church. It reflected our heart to share the unmerited favor of Christ with our City. We are still legally Grace Baptist Church (don't tell anyone) but now do business as Grace Seaford Church.

Not long after this change, a woman approached me at the church and let me know that she was very angry with me! She let me know that she was angry that I took Baptist out of our name. She wanted to know if we were still Baptist. I explained that we were never Baptist, but are Christians, who currently practice our faith within a Baptist church. She seemed confused and was not sure how to respond. So, she just pointed her finger at me and said, "Well I'm still mad with you". I just smiled and let her know that I was doing my best to prepare her for heaven where we will all be one under the name and banner of Christ and not any denomination.

---

[39] Kübler-Ross , Elisabeth. On Death and Dying: What the Dying Have to Teach Doctors, Nurses, Clergy and Their Own Families (p. 64). Scribner. Kindle Edition.

But I also let her know that we were still officially incorporated as Grace Baptist Church, which seemed to appease her denominational rant.

Kübler-Ross asserts that "Anger is a necessary stage of the healing process [...]", furthermore that the "more you truly feel it, the more it will begin to dissipate and the more you will heal." [40] While there is truth that anger needs expression, I have learned that anger is only one shade of many different and various emotions that people experience with the death of their church or loved one.

I have pastored many Christians who never experience anger and it is not because they are stuck in denial. Their perspective on God's sovereignty leads them to skip anger and experience other nuances of emotions previously described or move to another phase of their grief. However, it does not mean that those who do experience anger are somehow less spiritual. "The truth is that anger has no limits. It can extend not only to your friends, the doctors, your family, yourself, and your loved one who died, but also to God." [41] This is the place I found myself as a pastor after my brother died.

I shared in the previous chapter regarding the circumstances of my brother's death, but I did not share with you the anger I eventually felt toward God. The five stages of grief are fluid. If you have previously studied the Five Stages of Grief, then you know that they do not necessarily happen in sequential order. "As helpful as it may be to learn about these stages, they are not neatly packaged states that a person experiences sequentially; rather, they are a cycle, and the bereaved may experience more than one at a time." [42]

When my brother was sick and eventually dying, I spoke to God about several things. I reminded Him that I had never asked for anything from Him and had faithfully left a lucrative engineering career to enter the ministry. I reminded Him

---

[40] Kübler-Ross, Elisabeth; Kessler, David. On Grief and Grieving: Finding the Meaning of Grief Through the Five Stages of Loss (p. 12). Scribner. Kindle Edition.

[41] Kübler-Ross, Elisabeth; Kessler, David. On Grief and Grieving: Finding the Meaning of Grief Through the Five Stages of Loss (p. 13). Scribner. Kindle Edition.

[42] Clinton, T., & Hawkins, R. (2009). *The Quick-Reference Guide to Biblical Counseling: Personal and Emotional Issues* (p. 131). Baker Books.

of this because I was asking for miraculous healing for my brother. I knew that God was capable of the miraculous and I had seen Him heal in that way on several occasions. I also knew that His choice to heal was dependent upon His sovereignty and not on mine. So, I was angry with Him when He chose not to heal my brother. I experienced bargaining before anger, but the anger came the day after his passing.

I related perfectly with what Kübler-Ross shared about the dimension of bargaining with God. "Perhaps when our loved one was dying and we already experienced the bargaining stage, we asked God to intervene and save our loved one. Now after the loved one has died, we are left with a God who, in our eyes, did not come to our aid when we needed him the most." [43] That was exactly how I felt, and it was compounded by my present sacrifice of service to the Gospel of Christ.

I would sit in my front room in my home for days, with my brother's jacket around me, crying and yelling at God and letting Him know how mad I was at Him. Ironically, the closer you are to the Lord the more intense the emotion of anger can be. I "allow[ed myself] to feel and speak out the anger [and I learned …] that […] God is strong enough to handle [my] anger, strong enough to feel compassion and love for [me], even in the midst of" my anger aimed toward Him. [44] I also learned that instead of withdrawing from me, He drew closer to me in the midst of my anger. His presence was palpable at times. You see our God "heals the brokenhearted and binds up their wounds." [45] That is what the church needs to do when it experiences the tough emotions associated with the loss of their beloved church.

The reality is that "Death is unfair. Anger is a natural reaction to the unfairness of loss. Unfortunately, anger can isolate you from friends and family at the precise time you may need them the most." [46] When the congregants lash out at one another, the

[43] Kübler-Ross, Elisabeth; Kessler, David. On Grief and Grieving: Finding the Meaning of Grief Through the Five Stages of Loss (p. 13). Scribner. Kindle Edition.

[44] Kübler-Ross, Elisabeth; Kessler, David. On Grief and Grieving: Finding the Meaning of Grief Through the Five Stages of Loss (p. 15). Scribner. Kindle Edition.

[45] *The Holy Bible: English Standard Version* (Ps 147:3). (2016). Crossway Bibles.

[46] Kübler-Ross, Elisabeth; Kessler, David. On Grief and Grieving: Finding the Meaning of Grief Through the Five Stages of Loss (p. 16). Scribner. Kindle Edition.

pastor, or the community it may be that they are just venting their anger at the loss of the church that is so dear to them. It would be easy to withdraw from those who are expressing these intense emotions and that would be a mistake. "The tragedy is perhaps that we do not think of the reasons for [the congregants'] anger and take it personally, when it has originally nothing or little to do with the people who become the target of the anger." [47] We typically vent on those closest to us. So, that means that there is trust built between you and that person or that person and their God as they express anger or other emotions that go with loss.

What most people are looking for when they express anger is to have "several needs [...] met. [They need a safe place to be even] hostile and demanding without judgment and personal feelings about it. [They want to be] understood rather than judged." [48] The leader in this case must take the high road They must be professional, during confusion and loss. We must guard ourselves from becoming defensive or being unwilling to listen to people's objections to change. We need to understand how "our tolerance of the [their] rational or irrational anger [assists them to move forward with their grief]. We can do this only if we do not become defensive. We must learn to listen to [them] and at times even to accept some irrational anger, knowing that their relief in expressing it will help them toward a better acceptance". [49]

Their "anger is just another indication of the intensity of [their] love." [50] Their expressed anger or emotion shows how much they love their church, how much they feel connected to it, and the emotional investment they placed in its life and people. Our grief expressed through "Anger affirms that [we] can feel, that [we] did love,

---

[47] Kübler-Ross , Elisabeth. On Death and Dying: What the Dying Have to Teach Doctors, Nurses, Clergy and Their Own Families (p. 65). Scribner. Kindle Edition.

[48] Kübler-Ross , Elisabeth. On Death and Dying: What the Dying Have to Teach Doctors, Nurses, Clergy and Their Own Families (p. 90). Scribner. Kindle Edition.

[49] Kübler-Ross , Elisabeth. On Death and Dying: What the Dying Have to Teach Doctors, Nurses, Clergy and Their Own Families (p. 67). Scribner. Kindle Edition.

[50] Kübler-Ross, Elisabeth; Kessler, David. On Grief and Grieving: Finding the Meaning of Grief Through the Five Stages of Loss (p. 16). Scribner. Kindle Edition.

and that [we] have lost." [51] I was angry with God, because I loved my brother, so much, I missed him so much and I loved my God so much. This kind of anger needs to have a place to be vented, to be expressed, without judgment.

As you identify those expressing anger over the loss of what was, take time to engage them in various ways. Have them come by and vent over coffee at the church or take them out to lunch. While listening, don't become defensive. If you struggle with becoming defensive, try and learn how to become an active listener. "Active listening also leads to seeing things from the other person's point of view—almost always a helpful exercise." [52] Because it is an exercise, it can be learned and effectively employed by anyone, even me.

I am naturally a very defensive person and can levy a quick argument. It is part of my personality and gifting. You must be able to make a good argument if you are going to be an effective preacher. After all, what we present is an argument for life change every week. My personality type is DI on the DISC model (see www.discprofile.com) and my primary leadership style is Pioneering: "Pioneering leaders cut through the brush and inspire the group to venture into uncharted territory. They have a natural passion to grow, expand, and explore." [53]

[51] Kübler-Ross, Elisabeth; Kessler, David. On Grief and Grieving: Finding the Meaning of Grief Through the Five Stages of Loss (p. 16). Scribner. Kindle Edition.

[52] Shelley, M. (1986). *Helping those who don't want help* (Vol. 7, p. 140). Christianity Today, Inc.; Word Books.

[53] Scullard, Mark; Wilhelm, Emma; Sugerman, Jeffrey. The 8 Dimensions of Leadership: DiSC Strategies for Becoming a Better Leader (p. 39). Berrett-Koehler Publishers. Kindle Edition.

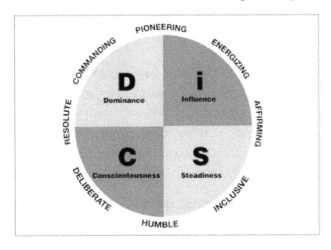

Figure 2.1. The DISC® Model [54]

Every personality comes with a primary leadership modality and with that both strengths and weaknesses. The problem with a pioneering leader is, "At times, they can err on the side of one-way communication. [55] My natural inclination is to listen long enough to figure out what is flawed in your argument, load my verbal gun, and prepare my salvo to sink your argument; so, we can move on and accomplish the vision! Knowing this about myself allowed me to see my need to learn the discipline of active listening. It was not easy, but I was able to learn it and exercise it well. I share this with you because if I can learn this skill, you can too!

Once you have heard the person vent their argument using active listening, let them know you are going to seriously consider and pray about what they have shared. Many times, in that short season of prayer and meditation you may find a compromise or concession you can give that moves your God-inspired vision forward but gives an incremental step that helps your congregant buy into what you

---

[54] Scullard, Mark; Wilhelm, Emma; Sugerman, Jeffrey. The 8 Dimensions of Leadership: DiSC Strategies for Becoming a Better Leader (p. 22). Berrett-Koehler Publishers. Kindle Edition.

[55] Scullard, Mark; Wilhelm, Emma; Sugerman, Jeffrey. The 8 Dimensions of Leadership: DiSC Strategies for Becoming a Better Leader (p. 40). Berrett-Koehler Publishers. Kindle Edition.

are envisioning. Because they were heard, they know that you value them, and you gain relational credibility for future change.

While it is true that we need to give space for anger to be expressed, others grieve with anger from an unhealthy perspective. Many times, the loss is not the loss of the church or God's missional advance, but a personal loss of power or comfort. Where this type of anger is expressed, it is only destructive and must be confronted. It is interesting that in grief research the people that expressed the type of anger are the ones that have the greatest narcissism.

"In that respect, the rich and successful, the controlling VIP is perhaps the poorest under these circumstances, as he is to lose the very things that made life so comfortable for him." [56] You will encounter this type of unrighteous anger in your church as you begin to implement change. This type of anger is connected to narcissistic grief. It is the fear of losing power and control. While this anger is very real in the lives of people who are dying, or those who are grieving, it is an unhealthy type of anger within the church seeking to die to self so that Christ's church can be resurrected. How do you confront and deal with this unhealthy anger? Certainly not in the same way that you deal with a healthy expression of anger where you create a place for its expression and understanding.

I'll never forget the woman who came to me angry about something I said early on about change. To give you some background and context, this was a well-published author who was intelligent and well-read. She had been a long-standing member and to be fair was a wonderful and amazing servant of Christ. But all of us can lose our way if we focus on the wrong things. I learned that many within the church had made the building, as well as the office of pastor, an idol. This understanding opposed some of our changes regarding how to use the whole of the property to reach families with young children.

There was an inner sanctum that was the previous pastor's office. It even had a moat-like design and employed a secretarial parlor that prohibited the congregants from gaining open access without an appointment. It reminded me of some of the

---

[56] Kübler-Ross , Elisabeth. On Death and Dying: What the Dying Have to Teach Doctors, Nurses, Clergy and Their Own Families (p. 69). Scribner. Kindle Edition.

Pentagon offices and layouts I had seen in my previous military career. In the first few months of introducing the need for change, I sensed that this issue (allocation of office space) had risen to the level of a sacred cow (Exodus 32). I have learned that sacred cows are opportunities to make sacred hamburgers. So, I decided to address this idol to gain momentum to grind up future more tenuous pieces of carnality.

I declared in a Sunday message that I did not need an office and was willing to set it aside my office for the sake of our children's program. I was willing to work using a laptop and give up all office space if it helped us to reach families and that children were more than welcome to have my office as well as the moat encircling it. My persnickety, fellow author came to me soon after that proclamation and declared that giving up the pastor's office was beneath my station and that I should repent and change my public declaration of submittal to the children's program. What's a pastor to do?

If you have not learned yet that the pulpit is the tiller of the ecclesiastical ship, then you need to draw from this example. You can steer from the helm or allow passengers to steer from steerage. And the reality is the North Star of Christ is always focused on the mission and not on fame, station, or status.

Therefore, the next Sunday I found a place in the message to double down on my desire to give away the pastor's office against the objections of many established critics. This woman was incensed, and she made a beeline for me right after the close of the service. She met me in the parking lot as I was leaving the church and let me know that she was outraged at my bringing up this issue from the pulpit. She was angry with me and as a result, would not be attending the church for the next four weeks to punish and discipline me as her pastor. Internally I did not know whether to shout for joy or just smile.

I let her know that I loved her and valued her feedback. Furthermore, I looked forward to seeing her return in four weeks. Additionally, I hoped she would return and enjoy the new children's area and her Pastor's surrendering of his office. She made a guttural noise, put her car in drive and almost ran over me. But to her credit and integrity, four weeks later she returned and gave me a hug! I learned to love this woman despite our differences on this issue and I believe that she ultimately fell more in love with our mutual stubbornness.

A few years later she came down with a terminal illness and I visited her with one of our deacons. I offered to anoint her with oil, which she was unfamiliar with, and offer a prayer based on James 5:14-16. She said she was open to the experience and would appreciate the pastoral prayer. I anointed my sister with oil and we prayed. We prayed together and neither of us recalled the situation that brought her anger. We both were simply left with our mutual humility before Jesus as fellow beggars who had been blessed to share in his provision!

If you have someone who is expressing anger from a place of an unhealthy place, there needs to be a confrontation to address that anger. After my leadership saw I, as well as our struggling sister, were willing to confront anger they all grew in their courage to move forward. Over time, our church ceased to use anger as a weapon when they saw that it did not help them to exercise influence.

Ensure in this phase that you allow for the proper expression of those grieving the loss of the church that used to expand the Kingdom. Go out of your way to way to exercise humility and active listening to ensure that those venting know they are heard and valued. While doing this, be careful to discern the difference between healthy and unhealthy anger.

Those within the church that are expressing unhealthy anger, because they just want their way or are making a power play, need to be confronted. Remember, if God has called you to lead then healthy confrontation is a part of that. If you struggle with confrontation, get some help from a good coach and do the hard work of confronting those who need to be confronted. Your church in the long run will thank you for being a good leader and you will move your church forward toward greater health. And I believe that most, but not all, will even appreciate your willingness to confront the issue while loving them despite their anger.

## NEXT STEPS

1. Ask your prayer team to pray and advise your leadership on how you can create a safer environment for people to vent their emotions about the state of the church. Implement suggested changes in your OFF-SUNDAY congregational gathering.

2. Increase your self-awareness by taking a DISC profile test. It is also good practice to have any high-level leaders serving near you take the test. While there are free DISC profile tests out there I prefer to use this website: https://discpersonalitytesting.com/

3. If you struggle with Active Listening read this article and implement changes that will help you become a better active listener: https://hbr.org/2021/12/how-to-become-a-better-listener

4. Once your DISC reports are completed, use them to gain perspective on your team. Write down how you might better interact with different people for better communication in your journal. Use the report to also gain better self-awareness.

# 6

# Bargaining

*[32] Then he said, "Oh let not the Lord be angry, and I will speak again but this once. Suppose ten are found there." He answered, "For the sake of ten I will not destroy it."*[57]

*Before a loss, it seems you will do anything if only your loved one may be spared. "Please, God," you bargain, "I will never be angry at my wife again if you'll just let her live."* [58]

I have enjoyed haggling all my life! I know that it is a lost art in the United States, but whenever I get on the mission field there is something about finding a good deal as well as the verbal art of knowing how to haggle and bargain that satisfies my soul as well as my pocket. But, when we get into the bargaining phase of grief, we are talking about a different kind of bargaining with a different purpose.

When connected to grief, "bargaining is really an attempt to postpone; it has to include a prize offered "for good behavior," it also sets a self-imposed "deadline" (e.g., one more performance, the son's wedding), and it includes an implicit promise that the patient will not ask for more if this one postponement is granted." [59] To better understand bargaining within a dying church, you need to study it from a biblical narrative and then connect that narrative in application to the modern

---

[57] *The Holy Bible: English Standard Version* (Ge 18:32). (2016). Crossway Bibles.

[58] Kübler-Ross, Elisabeth; Kessler, David. On Grief and Grieving: Finding the Meaning of Grief Through the Five Stages of Loss (p. 17). Scribner. Kindle Edition.

[59] Kübler-Ross , Elisabeth. On Death and Dying: What the Dying Have to Teach Doctors, Nurses, Clergy and Their Own Families (p. 96). Scribner. Kindle Edition.

church. Let's take a brief look at it from Abraham's encounter with God as he bargained for God to not destroy the city of Sodom.

We find this great exchange in Genesis 18:16–33. If you are unfamiliar or need to be refreshed regarding the story, Abraham appeals to God's sense of justice when he enquires if God will "sweep away the righteous with the wicked?" [60] He then starts a bargaining, or haggling process, regarding how many righteous people need to be found. The process descends from 50 all the way down to 10. The Lord entertains this process, even down to 10, and declares that "For the sake of ten I will not destroy it." [61] If God is all-knowing, and He is, then He already knew how many righteous people were in the city and He knew the outcome. So, what was the reason for Him entertaining the bargaining phase with Abraham?

"Bargaining can be an important reprieve from pain that occupies one's grief [... even if they] never believed the bargaining [and] just found relief in it momentarily." [62] God is patient with us through this process, and even though He knows the outcome, He is willing to journey with us through our bargaining phase. This speaks to the Lord's compassion as well as His incarnational desire to know us and be known by us. It is a quality that we need to embrace if we are to help our churches, and those within them, to move beyond bargaining to see the Lord's sovereign process and design.

Embracing this kind of incarnational compassion is not easy. It requires you and your leadership team to navigate the "what if" game. As we play the game, "We become lost in a maze of 'if only . . .' or 'What [if]. . .' statements. [You realize that the church] want[s] life returned to what it was [. . . as they conjecture] if only, if only, if only." [63] The bargaining phase for the church can manifest in many "what if" dimensions. In the chapter entitled "The Change Process & Grief", I

---

[60] *The Holy Bible: English Standard Version* (Ge 18:23). (2016). Crossway Bibles.

[61] *The Holy Bible: English Standard Version* (Ge 18:32). (2016). Crossway Bibles.

[62] Kübler-Ross, Elisabeth; Kessler, David. On Grief and Grieving: Finding the Meaning of Grief Through the Five Stages of Loss (p. 19). Scribner. Kindle Edition.

[63] Kübler-Ross, Elisabeth; Kessler, David. On Grief and Grieving: Finding the Meaning of Grief Through the Five Stages of Loss (p. 17). Scribner. Kindle Edition.

mentioned a church that believed that they were not growing because they did not have enough letters for their church sign. At the heart of this statement is bargaining. What do you do with these kinds of "what if" assertions from a dying church?

In this case, I was working with a denominational leader to coach this church. We both were initially in awe that they really believed this was a core issue for reaching people in their community. Especially since they were a rural church with low traffic that passed by their property. However, we realized that purchasing the missing letters was a small price to pay to help them navigate this bargain. Additionally, it would help us to build a greater relationship of trust as we helped them work through larger issues down the road. I'm sure you have already guessed that after we purchased the letters, the church did not grow substantially or come back to life. In fact, there was no measurable change in health. While this issue was quick and easy, other aspects of bargaining can be nuanced and more intense.

When I arrived at my current church, there was a great desire to reach out to everyone who had left the church during its years of decline. This is quite common for those who are the remnant, those who have stayed faithful to the dying church. They have a desire to regain the lost relationships with those who left. Especially, if the church is now on a trajectory to perceived health. The problem is you will rarely see someone return to a church that has been revitalized for several reasons.

The person who left is now connected to a new fellowship and they have built new relationships that they are unwilling to abandon for the possibility of returning to their previous church. If they left to pursue greater children's, youth, or Sunday programming then they will be unwilling to disengage with the new church they are now attending. The truth is "The more vocal members usually left the church [and] The comfortable members remained behind for the deathwatch". [64] Even though I knew this, and had experienced it in two previous revitalizations, I also knew the emotional dynamic for the existing members.

---

[64] Rainer, Thom S.. Autopsy of a Deceased Church: 12 Ways to Keep Yours Alive (Location: 354) . B&H Publishing Group. Kindle Edition.

They would not be able to move forward with the new vision for the church until they were able to work through this aspect of bargaining. In many ways, there is nobility in this aspect of bargaining. The existing congregants did not want to leave anyone behind and truly cared for those who used to attend. Therefore, we sent out a letter to all previous members and attenders of the church who were on the role.

In the letter we let them know that our Deacons were throwing a party in their honor on a specific Sunday, that we would love to see them return if they were disconnected from a local church, and that if they were connected to another church we would like to know how to pray for their new fellowship. Out of the hundreds of letters we sent out we saw no one return. However, we did get a handful of appreciative return letters telling us how to pray for their new church and how appreciative they were that someone checked in on them. Once this phase of "what if" was dispelled the church was able to move beyond this bargaining chip. An additional benefit is that we had a cleaned-up role that we could begin to work from.

As you traverse the bargaining phase, remain alert as to other phases of grief that the church may move in and out of as its bargaining chips come up short. They may feel angry or fall into depression once the truth hits them that their bargaining is not working.

> People often think of the stages as lasting weeks or months. They forget that the stages are responses to feelings that can last for minutes or hours as we flip in and out of one and then another. We do not enter and leave each individual stage in a linear fashion. We may feel one, then another, and back again to the first one. [65]

It is for this reason that you need to be ready to adjust as you discern the church slipping into a different phase. Because of the complexity of the bargaining phase, it may be useful to connect with a local denominational leader or a consultant.

Based on this complexity you may find it "helpful to have an interdisciplinary approach in [your] care, as the [pastor you will] often [be] the first one to hear about

---

[65] Kübler-Ross, Elisabeth; Kessler, David. On Grief and Grieving: Finding the Meaning of Grief Through the Five Stages of Loss (p. 18). Scribner. Kindle Edition.

such concerns." [66] While the church may trust you to shepherd them, to preach and teach they also may struggle to see you as the one to lead them through this difficult time. They may not believe that you have the administrative or leadership skills to lead through this difficult situation. While you very well may have the needed expertise, exercise humility, and bring in a consultant or leading expert in an area where bargaining is holding the church back from moving forward in their grief. The worst thing that will happen is that the consultant will more than likely agree with your assessment or offer a new insight.

In 2015, I was walking my church through many changes that needed to happen in structure and programming. While I have a master's in leadership, and had been a part of leading two previous churches through similar changes, they were pushing back hard and coming up with multiple bargaining options to deflect needed changes. If you're like me, you're reading all the time to grow and learn. The previous year I had picked up a great book on revitalization from Shannon O'Dell. Many of the changes I was promoting were anchored in the need for our church to change our culture so we could be more effective in reaching the lost within our community.

Shannon shared my conviction in this area of revitalizing the church. He shared in his book "that people say they want to reach the lost, until we start changing things they are familiar and comfortable with in order to do what it takes to really reach the lost." [67] So, I reached out to Shannon and brought him in over a weekend to talk with my leadership. He shared almost the exact same things I shared with the church, but because he was perceived as an external consultant and expert, they were able to move past their bargaining and embrace the needed changes for us to move forward. While this required me to set aside my pride and spend a few dollars for a consultant (Shannon was very generous with us) it was worth it to move the church past this phase.

---

[66] Kübler-Ross , Elisabeth. On Death and Dying: What the Dying Have to Teach Doctors, Nurses, Clergy and Their Own Families (p. 96). Scribner. Kindle Edition.

[67] O'Dell, Shannon. Transforming Church in Rural America (p. 73). Master Books. Kindle Edition.

You must be careful as bargains are presented. You need to remain receptive without embracing the wrong agendas that will not bring permanent change or renewal to your church. The bargaining process is generally one that does not bear fruit. "Why is bargaining often such a futile process? Because it is too little too late. If some welcome change comes, it is often temporary and the [church or person] is right back" where they started. [68] You may wonder or ask, then what is the ultimate purpose of bargaining?

There is a parallel to bargaining within the marital union that may help us understand the purpose of bargaining in its broader purpose within grief. As a couple works through bargaining they often must work on areas of compromise and use bargaining as a process to arrive at a healthy place. But what happens when only one within the relationship is willing to compromise or bargain? What is the point? "The key is to explore the situation and satisfy ourselves that we have done everything possible either to reverse the separation and divorce or to limit the damage. After that is done, we need to let the relationship go." [69]

In other words, bargaining allows a person as well as a church to think through all they could have done or should have done. When they have exhausted all the "what ifs" and "maybes" they then can move to the next phase and entertain a possibility that is entirely new and is not anchored necessarily in the church that was but the church that will be. "Throughout the entire process, we should be true to our convictions and treat others evenhandedly. " [70]

Try to remember that if a church is very sick, or actively dying, there is a little chance that you will bring health and at most you or a consultant may be able to extend the life, or death process, but not bring long-term healing. It is not that they do not want to or that they do not have the best tools or technology, it is because they are

[68] Kniskern, J. W. (1993). *When the vow breaks: a survival and recovery guide for Christians facing divorce* (p. 32). Broadman & Holman Publishers.

[69] Kniskern, J. W. (1993). *When the vow breaks: a survival and recovery guide for Christians facing divorce* (p. 33). Broadman & Holman Publishers.

[70] Kniskern, J. W. (1993). *When the vow breaks: a survival and recovery guide for Christians facing divorce* (p. 33). Broadman & Holman Publishers.

working against the natural order of death, burial, and resurrection. At some point, you have to move beyond bargaining and just face the facts.

Max Lucado in *God Came Near* has a chapter called "Facing the Facts". The book is an encouragement to all those facing difficult situations that God draws near in those times. In the same chapter, he shared this principle in a succinct and relatable way:

> And the reminder is sobering. This is a hospital. The sole function of this building is to bargain with death. The walls can't be white enough nor the staff polite enough to hide the stark reality of the bottom line: People come here to give all they have to postpone the inevitable.
>
> We give it our best shot. We put up the best we have—the best technology, the best minds, the best equipment; and yet, at best we walk away with an extension, never a solution. And though we may walk or be wheeled out with smiles and waves of victory, down deep we know it is just a matter of time until the best we have won't be enough and the enemy will conquer." [71]
>
> Your church's bargaining is their way of trying to forestall the inevitable and draw out one more season of holding on to the church they have become accustomed to and comfortable attending. "But this obsession with fleeing the facts is as maddening as it is futile. For, as in the case of the hospital, the truth always surfaces. A siren sounds causing reality to shock us out of our sleep." [72]

Lead and shepherd them through the bargaining to find the truth. We must come through the death of what was if we are to experience all that God has for us. Be reminded that while God is patient and loving with our bargaining; ultimately, He cannot be bargained with because He is omniscient and already knows the outcome.

---

[71] Lucado, M. (1987). *God came near: chronicles of the Christ* (p. 127). Multnomah Press.

[72] Lucado, M. (1987). *God came near: chronicles of the Christ* (p. 129). Multnomah Press.

"God is not a bargaining God. You cannot barter with Him. You must do business with Him on His own terms." [73]

God's terms are to come to Him, take up your cross, and crucify the old life so that a new resurrected body can be reborn for a new generation and new season. Know that it will be hard but that denying the truth through battling only prolongs the church's death. Also, be encouraged that Jesus meets us in these difficult moments if we will call and rely upon him instead of man's wisdom to merely prolong the inevitable. When you "find yourself alone in a dark alley facing the undeniables of life, don't cover them with a blanket, or ignore them with a nervous grin. Don't turn up the TV and pretend they aren't there. Instead, stand still, whisper [Christ's] name, and listen. He is nearer than you think." [74]

Christ stands ready to walk with you to the cross, into the tomb, and out to rise in resurrection. He has been there before, and He knows how you feel. He too bargained in the Garden of Gethsemane for a different path that would lead away from the pain of the cross. But through prayer, faith, and obedience He cut through the bargaining to arrive at "not my will, but yours, be done." [75]

This is what you ultimately want for your church, your ministry, and your Lord. That your church would present their bargain, pray through to the truth, and then follow Christ into an obedient death in hopeful expectation of a resurrection not of your making but His. I'm praying for you and churches all over our world that they would follow our Savior into the crucified life and throw off every commercial bargain promising temporary relief.

---

[73] Lucado, M. (1996). *Life lessons from the inspired word of God: book of Romans* (p. 30). Word Pub.

[74] Lucado, M. (1987). *God came near: chronicles of the Christ* (p. 131). Multnomah Press.

[75] *The Holy Bible: English Standard Version* (Lk 22:42). (2016). Crossway Bibles.

## NEXT STEPS

1. When you meet with your prayer team, ask them about any areas where the church has expressed bargaining where they are being kept from moving forward. Write these in your journal and then pray for each one with your team.

2. Based on feedback from your prayer team, discern which bargains you need to address and what you think will be probable outcomes after addressing them. Manage expectations by clearly communicating with the church why you are addressing the specific issue and what you believe will be the outcome.

3. Build a team to address each unique bargain. The people who brought up the bargain should be added to that team. If they are unwilling to serve, then move on to a different bargaining issue. Keep in mind that there is a big difference between a complainer and someone who is invested in the church.

4. Equip the team with all they need. After you address the bargain, debrief with the team and encourage them regardless of the outcome. If you are wrong and you find addressing a specific bargain brings momentum toward a certain part of the church admit it and invest in what God is blessing. If the bargain fails, then encourage the church that you tried and now it is time to move forward.

5. Reach out to a trusted consultant for issues where you sense that the church needs an external voice to address a specific area of bargaining. Bring them in to meet with your team or church.

6. As you continue to meet with your prayer team, ask if the church is digressing into other areas of expressing their grief. Pray over each area listed and address where appropriate.

7. Continue to journal on each of the bargaining areas.

*Pastor Larry Davis*

# 7

# Depression

*²⁸ Come to me, all who labor and are heavy laden, and I will give you rest. ²⁹ Take my yoke upon you, and learn from me, for I am gentle and lowly in heart, and you will find rest for your souls. ⁷⁶*

*The dull depression he experienced in a somnolent condition at first gave him a little relief, but only as something new, afterwards it became as distressing as the pain itself or even more so. ⁷⁷*

It is hard for us to fathom that depression has any function other than to mentally wound or hurt a person. Therefore, the common response is to try and cheer someone up. But to properly deal with depression you need to understand its purpose within the context of grief. "The term *depression* may be used to describe a normal reaction to loss, a symptom of a disorder, or the disorder itself." ⁷⁸ We tend to look at depression from a similar and flat definition, but there are several forms that it can take. It is beyond the scope of this book to address all the various forms of depression and their nuances.

If someone is clinically depressed, with no specific situation that is connected to their mood or state of mind, then they need to be referred to someone who can professionally and medically treat them. However, "[I]n grief, depression is a way for nature to keep us protected by shutting down the nervous system so that we can

---

⁷⁶ *The Holy Bible: English Standard Version* (Mt 11:28–29). (2016). Crossway Bibles.

⁷⁷ Tolstoy, L. (1886). *The Death of Ivan Ilych (p. 40)*. United States: Seven Treasure Publications.

⁷⁸ Al, I.-I. (1999). Culture and Psychopathology. In D. G. Benner & P. C. Hill (Eds.), *Baker encyclopedia of psychology & counseling* (2nd ed., p. 309). Baker Books.

adapt to something we feel we cannot handle." [79] Within depression brought on by grief, there are typically two types of depression: reactive and preparatory.

To be transparent, these two forms of depression were difficult to assimilate into the church paradigm. When leading a church through the depression phase you are dealing with both corporate and individual forms of depression. How and where do preparatory and reactive depression fit? Is one or both applicable to a church grieving or is one or both better fitted to individual grieving? To better understand and answer these questions, I reached out to a former professor: Dr. Ron Cobb at Luther Rice Seminary.

Dr. Cobb is well trained in Biblical Counseling and is an authority not only on this issue within counseling but also well trained theologically (B.S., Columbia Bible College; M.A.S., University of Alabama Huntsville; M.Div., New Orleans Baptist Theological Seminary; M.A., Luther Rice Seminary; D.Min., Southern Baptist Theological Seminary; Ph.D., Northcentral University). Additionally, he has pastored at the local church level and was able to conceptualize with me how grieving works within a dying church because he also has pastored within those contexts. More specifically, it was the merger of his counseling discipline with his theological training where I was looking for great insight.

When we met, he first encouraged me how needed this book is within the local church. He was excited to be able to help with defining depression contextually within a dying church and he began by giving me his definition for both reactive and preparatory depression. Dr. Cobb defined reactive depression as "a disorder that is triggered by a traumatic event, stressful event, stressful situation, or an external problem beyond".

He then defined preparatory depression as "the type of grief people who are dying go through". When I asked him about how these two forms of depression work within the context of a church, he explained that it was his opinion that reactive depression is a corporate expression and that preparatory is an individual one. He went on to explain that both the individual (preparatory) and the collective

---

[79] Kübler-Ross, Elisabeth; Kessler, David. On Grief and Grieving: Finding the Meaning of Grief Through the Five Stages of Loss (p. 21). Scribner. Kindle Edition.

congregation (reactive) are processing both forms of grief. This formed my axiom for how I wanted to better understand how to lead a church through this phase both corporately and personally.

Within reactive depression, your church is reacting to a consequence of the impending death of the church. An example of reactive depression from Kübler-Ross' research would include "the added loss of a job due to many absences or the inability to function, and mothers and wives may have to become the breadwinners, thus depriving the children of the attention they previously had." [80] These losses evoke a depression based on how the loss or sickness generates specific consequences. Therefore, they require a pragmatic approach that addresses the consequence of loss from a therapeutic place to gain perspective within the social construct of the corporate church life.

Reactive expression for the church would be how communal life is impacted by the impending death of the church. The reduction of the budget based on reduced giving, changes in corporate worship based on a lack of volunteers, or the loss of a vital or endearing program would be a few examples. While these losses are corporate, they impact individuals as well as the general mood of the church. How do you shepherd through reactive depression?

In the instance of the loss of finance, you will have to adjust spending. You may have to adjust staffing or salaries. A full-time pastor may have to consider becoming bi-vocational. In the example of corporate worship, the church may have to use CDs, tracks, or even rely less on music and more on prayer and scripture reading in the public gathering (not necessarily a bad thing to have to navigate). Vital programs will have to be pragmatically assessed and determine if they are necessary for the current church or if they were designed for a past era. But, in all these examples you are being extremely pragmatic in how you lead and address the root issue connected to reactionary depression.

Conversely, preparatory depression "is the preparatory grief that the terminally ill patient has to undergo in order to prepare himself for his final separation from this

---

[80] Kübler-Ross, Elisabeth. On Death and Dying: What the Dying Have to Teach Doctors, Nurses, Clergy and Their Own Families (p. 98). Scribner. Kindle Edition.

world." [81] Within the church context, this is the emotional response individuals process within the corporate gathering that their church is going to die. Preparatory depression is a necessary and emotionally draining phase that precedes acceptance. [82] This form of depression is not treated as much as it is navigated toward acceptance.

In this sense, preparatory "depression is a tool to prepare for the impending loss [...] in order to facilitate the state of acceptance [; therefore,] encouragements and reassurances are not as meaningful." [83] This is why hollow platitudes or false promises offered can be hurtful or devastating to those experiencing preparatory grief. Unfortunately, this is our typical response based on the monolithic way we understand and approach depression. If you are leading a church through this phase you "should know that this type of depression is necessary and beneficial if the [church] is to die in a stage of acceptance and peace." [84]

To serve and shepherd your church through this phase you will need to avoid grasping at programs that offer false hope or miracle cures. Be careful which consultants you lean into. Sniff out the used car salesmen who promise a church turnaround that does not require radical change and just tweaks in your structure or programming. You will need to embrace an understanding that the church is actively dying and that your role is to help them express and process their feelings of depression.

After all, "The loss of a loved one is a very depressing situation, and depression is a normal and appropriate response. To not experience depression after a loved one

---

[81] Kübler-Ross, Elisabeth. On Death and Dying: What the Dying Have to Teach Doctors, Nurses, Clergy and Their Own Families (p. 99). Scribner. Kindle Edition.

[82] Kübler-Ross, Elisabeth. On Death and Dying: What the Dying Have to Teach Doctors, Nurses, Clergy and Their Own Families (p. 98). Scribner. Kindle Edition.

[83] Kübler-Ross, Elisabeth. On Death and Dying: What the Dying Have to Teach Doctors, Nurses, Clergy and Their Own Families (p. 99). Scribner. Kindle Edition.

[84] Kübler-Ross, Elisabeth. On Death and Dying: What the Dying Have to Teach Doctors, Nurses, Clergy and Their Own Families (p. 100). Scribner. Kindle Edition.

dies would be unusual." [85] Therefore, it is normal for those within your church to feel depressed after they process that they did all they could do to save their church and now they are at a place where they know that it will eventually die. While the Kübler-Ross model offers little for this form of depression, the Christian Gospel offers great encouragement, if properly understood.

Earlier I shared that my brother died of a rare cancer at a young age. My mother also died of cancer at 65 years of age. I was only 26 at the time and because my mother's illness lasted a few months, I was able to experience both preparatory and reactive depression.

When my mother was actively dying (preparatory grief) there was little I could do other than ask God for a healing. However, with the reactionary grief, I had practical things that helped me to move forward with a new reality that was hard to accept. In fact, for those who are grieving the impending loss of someone they love or are processing their own terminal situation, empty platitudes and false hope are unwelcome.

Reaction to such empty offerings can evoke harsh responses. When I was processing my mother's impending death it was only the hope of the Gospel that gave me strength and hope anchored in the truth that Christ had conquered death and that because of His victory I would see her again. The promise of resurrection was paramount in helping me to accept her death. I really don't understand how unbelievers can even process grief without Christ's hope.

This hope came in the form of people being present with me, praying with me, and just reminding me that they loved me. The living presence of Christ was real within His Bride, the Church, and I was encouraged not through her words, but by her presence and love. Christ's bride loved me to acceptance and soothed my soul in my preparatory grief.

My wife and I were a part of a wonderful church in that season (Rockawalkin UMC) and the pastor there (Bill Sterling) knew how to love well! Because of my love for

---

[85] Kübler-Ross, Elisabeth; Kessler, David. On Grief and Grieving: Finding the Meaning of Grief Through the Five Stages of Loss (p. 21). Scribner. Kindle Edition.

music, I joined the choir and helped the newly formed praise team. On one Sunday in 1998, I was feeling particularly crushed in spirit regarding my mother's sickness and impending death. Pastor Bill opened the altar of the church for anyone who needed prayer that morning, and I knew I was in desperate need of God to touch my soul.

I had never been to the altar for prayer and was reluctant to draw any attention to myself; however, I also felt an incredible pull to go. I stepped out of the choir loft and somehow my feet found their way to the front of the altar where I kneeled in brokenness. I began to sense hands being placed on my shoulders and back, and Pastor Bill eventually prayed over me for God's love and healing to be manifest. I don't remember what he said exactly, but I could sense the living presence of Christ in that moment. I was undone while at the same time feeling His presence comforting me through His Bride. When I finally rose to my feet and looked behind me, over half the church was praying for me! As I recall this event even now, I can't help but weep and still be undone by the love of God through His Church!

Pastor Bill even visited my mother before she died and shared communion with our family. He taught me, by shepherding me through my grief, what a Pastor is and what they do. He is retired at the time of the writing of this book, but I still think of him as my pastor. He is one of the big reasons I went into vocational ministry, and I still enjoy meeting with him from time to time to just catch up on life. He had the wisdom to know he could not save me or my mom, but he knew One who had already saved us both. That kind of hope is the only cure for preparatory depression and grief.

After my mother passed, depression eventually came over me, and it was one of the harder phases for me personally. I am an upbeat person and have been blessed to not have to deal with clinical depression or other emotional swings. I share that so that you might understand that some are more susceptible to depression, and to help you understand that this phase did not at all feel natural or normal to me.

I truly love and embrace life, rising early every day, excited to take on the challenges that will come my way. But a few weeks after my mother's death I could not bring myself to even get out of bed. I was unprepared for the fact that those working through depression often "withdraw from life [and are] left in a fog of intense sadness, wondering, perhaps, if there is any point in going on alone."

[86] These emotions paralyzed me. I was working through the reactive elements of depression and was not sure how to navigate them. In that season, I cried out to God often. As time moved forward, I learned that "[17] When the righteous cry for help, the LORD hears and delivers them out of all their troubles. [moreover that] "[18] The LORD is near to the brokenhearted and saves the crushed in spirit." [87]

Maybe you have experienced some of those reactive moments: When you go to pick up the phone and realize mid-dial that your loved one is not on this side of eternity, and your mood sinks low. Or when your first child is born, and you realize your mother is not there to share in that moment. It is in these later reactive times that practical grief counseling, coping tools, and the continued loving presence of a healthy, local church mended my soul. So, what are the practical ways you can lead through reactive and preparatory depression for your church?

There is one common aspect that impacts both reactive and preparatory depression and that is HOPE! This is where the Kübler-Ross model does not always fully align practicality with a Christian worldview. This is not to say that the model does not bring great insight, but its use and understanding of HOPE is dynamically opposed to the Biblical idea of HOPE. It is the innate lack of hope that is missing in the depression phase that needs to be specifically augmented if we are to shepherd our church into biblical acceptance and see our church rebirthed.

Kübler-Ross' prescription is simply to do nothing other than be present and allow the dying to eventually come to the fatalistic reality that they will die so that they can accept it. Depression in this modality is viewed as the emotive state that helps to bring the person to acceptance of their fate. From their worldview:

> The patient is in the process of losing everything and everybody he loves. If he is allowed to express his sorrow he will find a final acceptance much

---

[86] Kübler-Ross, Elisabeth; Kessler, David. On Grief and Grieving: Finding the Meaning of Grief Through the Five Stages of Loss (p. 20-21). Scribner. Kindle Edition.

[87] *The Holy Bible: English Standard Version* (Psalm 34:17–18). (2016). Crossway Bibles.

easier, and he will be grateful to those who can sit with him during this stage of depression without constantly telling him not to be sad. [88]

As tough as it is, depression can be dealt with in a paradoxical way. See it as a visitor, perhaps an unwelcome one, but one who is visiting whether you like it or not. Make a place for your guest. Invite your depression to pull up a chair with you in front of the fire, and sit with it, without looking for a way to escape. Allow the sadness and emptiness to cleanse you and help you explore your loss in its entirety. When you allow yourself to experience depression, it will leave as soon as it has served its purpose in your loss. As you grow stronger, it may return from time to time, but that is how grief works. [89]

It is sad that Kübler-Ross missed what their own research discerned because their worldview lacked the truth of a Christian lens to focus the light of hope onto the darkness of depression's impact on the human soul. One of their study subjects (Mr. H.) shared with them that "What grieved him most, however, was the loss of hope." [90] When faced with a hopeless situation "Mr. H. did not give up and admitted himself to another hospital, where hope was offered." [91]

The human soul above all craves hope! In the Kübler-Ross model, a patient must suffer through depression which leads them to a hopeless finality that is beyond their control. Within the Christian faith, HOPE is what conquers both depression and death. For, "faith is the assurance of things hoped for, the conviction of things not seen." [92] Within this biblical truth lies the crux for the unbelieving world. Those

[88] Kübler-Ross , Elisabeth. On Death and Dying: What the Dying Have to Teach Doctors, Nurses, Clergy and Their Own Families (p. 99). Scribner. Kindle Edition.

[89] Kübler-Ross, Elisabeth; Kessler, David. On Grief and Grieving: Finding the Meaning of Grief Through the Five Stages of Loss (p. 22). Scribner. Kindle Edition.

[90] Kübler-Ross , Elisabeth. On Death and Dying: What the Dying Have to Teach Doctors, Nurses, Clergy and Their Own Families (p. 119). Scribner. Kindle Edition.

[91] Kübler-Ross , Elisabeth. On Death and Dying: What the Dying Have to Teach Doctors, Nurses, Clergy and Their Own Families (p. 119-120). Scribner. Kindle Edition.

[92] *The Holy Bible: English Standard Version* (Heb 11:1). (2016). Crossway Bibles.

who see no hope for the dying, or a dying church, show their unwillingness to frame things within a biblical worldview.

The paradox in this situation is how we define hope. Where Kübler-Ross' model aligns with the Christian worldview is regarding false hope. Many churches and people who cling to a false hope will be left unprepared to accept the death that God is allowing to happen. The problem is that Kübler-Ross sees faith more as a salve for the human soul as opposed to the ultimate cure. If you are a leader, attender, or pastor of a local church please hear clearly: THERE IS HOPE! But the depression phase within your church needs to finish its work so that your people can only see one ultimate hope for the resurrection of their church.

> The depression you are now feeling has a purpose if you will humbly search your soul. As difficult as it is to endure, depression has elements that can be helpful in grief. It slows us down and allows us to take real stock of the loss. It makes us rebuild ourselves from the ground up. It clears the deck for growth. It takes us to a deeper place in our soul that we would not normally explore. [93]

As you allow depression to sink, it is my hope that you and your church will come to a place of abject despair! I know that sounds crazy, but when the first church fully took in the gravity of the crucifixion, it crushed them emotionally. They were left understanding that they could do nothing to fix the situation, and their emotional state left them dependent on a miracle from God.

If this is where you are, then you are set up emotionally to finally do away with all the bargaining, anger, and games. As a leader remind your people that "It is the LORD who goes before you. He will be with you; he will not leave you or forsake you." [94] That means that He has a plan that leads you through the valley of death. But, to cling to where your church used to be will return the church back into the valley of death. You need to move *through* it and not get stuck *in it*. From this perspective Kübler-Ross is right, you need to allow depression to do its work. But

---

[93] Kübler-Ross, Elisabeth; Kessler, David. On Grief and Grieving: Finding the Meaning of Grief Through the Five Stages of Loss (p. 24). Scribner. Kindle Edition.

[94] *The Holy Bible: English Standard Version* (Dt 31:7–8). (2016). Crossway Bibles.

not because of death's fatalism which will prepare you for death, but for the resurrected life that follows. Not a life of your making or the congregants' making, but one that the Lord Himself will create.

Focus on preaching and teaching in this season on the resurrection of Christ and how God is calling the church to humbly submit in a posture of prayer and expectation. Remind them that "In the world you will have tribulation. But take heart; [Christ has] overcome the world." [95] He overcame this world in a way that no one could have ever conceived of prior to the crucifixion and resurrection. Teach through passages like Isaiah 43:17-19:

> [16] Thus says the LORD, who makes a way in the sea, a path in the mighty waters, [17] who brings forth chariot and horse, army and warrior; they lie down, they cannot rise, they are extinguished, quenched like a wick: [18] "Remember not the former things, nor consider the things of old. [19] Behold, I am doing a new thing; now it springs forth, do you not perceive it? I will make a way in the wilderness and rivers in the desert. [96]

Early on at my church, I preached through this message, and I called the sermon GLORY DAYS. Not only is that a great Springsteen song, but it is a message that reminds our church that we move forward through the process of dying to what *was* so that God can do a new thing. How many churches get stuck in the GLORY DAYS and lamenting over what was instead of seeking the King of Glory who desires a new work! Remind the church that hope is not in remembering the past, but seeing the one who continues to create new opportunities for hope!

It is not enough in this season to simply preach the truth: You must lead your church to spiritually be *infused* with the truth. Lead them through public moments of prayer based on passages like Proverbs 3:5-8:

> [5] Trust in the LORD with all your heart, and do not lean on your own understanding. [6] In all your ways acknowledge him, and he will make straight your paths. [7] Be not wise in your own eyes; fear the LORD, and turn

---

[95] *The Holy Bible: English Standard Version* (Jn 16:32–33). (2016). Crossway Bibles.

[96] *The Holy Bible: English Standard Version* (Is 43:16–19). (2016). Crossway Bibles.

away from evil. [8] It will be healing to your flesh and refreshment to your bones.[97]

Bring up this proverb in your leadership meetings (and others like it), your public services, and prayer meetings. Use each verse one at a time as a guided time of prayer. If you are unfamiliar with how to lead these kinds of prayer times or moments, check out ministries like *The 6:4 Fellowship* (*https://64fellowship.com/*). The power of prayer will soften your church's heart to receive what God is doing in allowing your church to die, while at the same time still seeing that there is a resurrection waiting for the church on the other side of its burial.

Remind the church that humility and being right with God are key to seeing the Lord deliver the church through the valley to the other side to experience resurrection. But when going through the valley the emotions will be real and depression has a purpose. "[19] Many are the afflictions of the righteous, but the LORD delivers him out of them all. [20] He keeps all his bones; not one of them is broken." [98] Psalm 34 reminds us that we need to have a righteous heart that does not seek our agenda but is connected to the Savior's agenda. Jesus has a purpose for your church! Therefore, there is HOPE! But to live out that hope, your church will have to traverse a DEATH and a BURIAL to be able to open the door when Jesus knocks, calling you from the grave to rise with Him to a new resurrected reality.

---

[97] *The Holy Bible: English Standard Version* (Pr 3:5–8). (2016). Crossway Bibles.

[98] *The Holy Bible: English Standard Version* (Ps 34:17–20). (2016). Crossway Bibles.

## NEXT STEPS

1. Meet with your prayer team and discuss how your church is expressing reactive and preparatory depression. Record their answers in your journal.

2. Speak to your prayer team as well as your church leadership about practical solutions to address the reactional elements.

3. Construct a message series that will focus your church on the HOPE of the resurrection. Connect that HOPE to the church's need to accept where they are and focus their prayer life to beg God to show what resurrection He would like to bring to your church.

4. Have your prayer team begin to lead more aspects of corporate prayer in the Sunday service. Reveal how you are sensing the Lord moving for a resurrection for the church and ask God in your public service for the courage to receive His will.

5. Continue to address specific bargains by implementing changes that you think are necessary for the church to see they do not work so that they can move beyond bargaining.

6. Update your journal on areas of bargaining. What are the outcomes? Have you communicated them to the church? In what ways have you been surprised or encouraged?

# 8

# Acceptance

*But we do not want you to be uninformed, brothers, about those who are asleep, that you may not grieve as others do who have no hope.*[99]

*"It is finished!" said someone near him. He heard these words and repeated them in his soul. "Death is finished," he said to himself. "It is no more!" He drew in a breath, stopped in the midst of a sigh, stretched out, and died.* [100]

So, we finally come to the final stage: acceptance. If our church, and those attending, reach this phase they will be "neither depressed nor angry about [their] 'fate.'" [101]The larger emotional place will be one of understanding the truth regarding the church's impending death. While it may seem that your work is done at this point, that could not be further from the truth. There is much to do if we are to properly prepare our church for the resurrection that we hope is coming. Additionally, we do not want our church to fall back into one of the previous grieving phases.

"Acceptance is not about liking a situation. It is about acknowledging all that has been lost and learning to live with that loss." [102] While there are great therapies and counseling techniques for the individual who is entering this phase of acceptance, there are three key values that will best assist you and your leadership team: GOD's

[99] *The Holy Bible: English Standard Version* (1 Th 4:13). (2016). Crossway Bibles.

[100] Tolstoy, L. (1886). *The Death of Ivan Ilych (p. 62-63)*. United States: Seven Treasure Publications.

[101] Kübler-Ross, Elisabeth. On Death and Dying: What the Dying Have to Teach Doctors, Nurses, Clergy and Their Own Families (p. 123). Scribner. Kindle Edition.

[102] Kübler-Ross, Elisabeth; Kessler, David. On Grief and Grieving: Finding the Meaning of Grief Through the Five Stages of Loss (p. 26). Scribner. Kindle Edition.

SOVERIGNTY, HOPE, and HUMILITY. I know that we already talked about the importance of hope regarding depression, but you will double down or amplify that message during this phase. That's because "The one thing that usually persists through all these stages is hope." [103] Before I present the practical aspects for leading through acceptance, let's spend just a few moments on better understanding this particular and unique phase.

One of the challenges in getting to acceptance (or navigating the grief process) is that it is not a normalized aspect of our life or church experience. "It might be helpful if more people would talk about death and dying as an intrinsic part of life just as they do not hesitate to mention when someone is expecting a new baby." [104] I recently rewrote our membership class, specifically the section on our church's history. I rewrote it from the perspective of the cycle of DEATH, BURIAL, and RESURRECTION. I share about our church's birth, childhood, adolescence, mature years, decline, and death.

I did this so that I could introduce a culture within our church that accepts that DEATH, BURIAL, and RESURRECTION are normative within those who follow Christ. Our people come into a living relationship when they die to the life they were living so that they can embrace the life they are called to. Think about this truth that is contained throughout the New Testament. "I have been crucified with Christ. It is no longer I who live, but Christ who lives in me. And the life I now live in the flesh I live by faith in the Son of God, who loved me and gave himself for me." [105] Death is normative here, and so is the resurrected life that follows.

Think about the living illustration within the ordinance of baptism and its connection to the death and resurrection of Christ! "We were buried therefore with him by baptism into death, in order that, just as Christ was raised from the dead by

---

[103] Kübler-Ross, Elisabeth. On Death and Dying: What the Dying Have to Teach Doctors, Nurses, Clergy and Their Own Families (p. 148). Scribner. Kindle Edition.

[104] Kubler-Ross, Elisabeth. On Death and Dying: What the Dying Have to Teach Doctors, Nurses, Clergy and Their Own Families (p. 150). Scribner. Kindle Edition.

[105] *The Holy Bible: English Standard Version* (Ga 2:20). (2016). Crossway Bibles.

the glory of the Father, we too might walk in newness of life." [106] These passages, and many more like them, show the consistent message of DEATH, BURIAL, and RESURRECTION as it pertains uniquely to the Christian experience and yet we constantly fail to reach the phase of acceptance throughout the United States. It is not normalized, and therefore it is harder for our people to accept because we as a Christian church have not consistently embraced the preaching of the cross.

A few years ago, my pastor (Bill Sterling) recommended that I read a book about the crucifixion written by Fleming Rutledge, who is an author and Episcopal Priest. Pastor Bill's recommendations have always taken me deeper into my Christian walk and calling as a pastor, and so I grabbed the book. I quickly realized why he recommended it: Rutledge articulated this very problem in the church as she confessionally shared the issue from her own tradition.

> In the Episcopal Church, the sermons and meditations that were the centerpieces of these services have now been largely replaced by prayers and litanies, substantial interludes of music, short homilies (optional), and liturgical practices such as reverencing the cross and receiving the reserved sacrament. This devaluation of the preaching of the cross is, I believe, a serious deprivation for those who seek to follow Jesus. [107]

Rutledge's comments reveal a common problem that is not limited to her denomination. Churches in North America have lost their focus on preaching the cross and the call to a crucified life. Because we are missing this within our culture, our people struggle with acceptance within the grieving process for the local church. This is why your messages and discipleship process must contain aspects of normalizing the cycle of DEATH, BURIAL, and RESURRECTION as a part of the Christian experience.

If you can create this cultural narrative (through preaching and discipleship) and normalize the crucified sequence, you will discover that "An accepted grief is a conquered grief; a conquered grief will very soon be a comforted grief; and a

---

[106] *The Holy Bible: English Standard Version* (Ro 6:4). (2016). Crossway Bibles.

[107] Rutledge, Fleming. The Crucifixion: Understanding the Death of Jesus Christ (Location 202). Wm. B. Eerdmans Publishing Co.. Kindle Edition.

comforted grief is a joy."[108] As a result, your church will begin: "Reorganizing their life, filling new roles, and reconnecting with those around them are all healthy and important facets of the healing process."[109] This season is not the season to share a new vision for where the church is headed.

Keep in mind that "Acceptance should not be mistaken for a happy stage. It is almost void of feelings. It is as if the pain had gone, the struggle is over, and there comes a time for 'the final rest before the long journey' as one patient phrased it." [110] Acceptance is preparing your church to accept the death that God is bringing about; not from an unguided fatalistic perspective, but from God's purposeful plan to bring you into DEATH, BURIAL, and RESURRECTION.

For you to help your church accept their impending death, they need to have a healthy, theological perspective on the sovereignty of God. This is not only true of the church, but also of those who accept their own mortality. "We will never like this reality or make it okay, but eventually we accept it. We learn to live with it. It is the new norm with which we must learn to live." [111]

"A holy and loving God has the right to be sovereign. Men have ever stumbled at the doctrine of God's sovereignty, chiefly because they have not understood it." [112] The reality you are training your church to theologically accept is that through God's sovereignty, He has allowed your church to die. This is a difficult but necessary aspect of accepting that God has allowed for our death in His larger plan to bring hope to His mission. Depending on your church's denomination, your training, and your theological lens you will lead through this uniquely.

---

[108] Exell, J. S. (n.d.). *Isaiah* (Vol. 3, p. 370). Fleming H. Revell Company.

[109] Clinton, T., & Hawkins, R. (2009). *The Quick-Reference Guide to Biblical Counseling: Personal and Emotional Issues* (p. 131). Baker Books.

[110] Kübler-Ross, Elisabeth. On Death and Dying: What the Dying Have to Teach Doctors, Nurses, Clergy and Their Own Families (p. 124). Scribner. Kindle Edition.

[111] Kübler-Ross, Elisabeth; Kessler, David. On Grief and Grieving: Finding the Meaning of Grief Through the Five Stages of Loss (p. 25). Scribner. Kindle Edition.

[112] Mullins, E. Y. (1908). *The Axioms of Religion: A New Interpretation of the Baptist Faith* (p. 79). The Griffith & Rowland Press.

So, that you can best understand how I led through this and helped my church understand it, I submit the following definition:

> The word means principal, chief, and supreme. It speaks first of position (God is the chief Being in the universe), then of power (God is supreme in power in the universe). How He exercises that power is revealed in the Scriptures. A sovereign could be a dictator (God is not), or a sovereign could abdicate the use of his powers (God has not). Ultimately God is in complete control of all things, though He may choose to let certain events happen according to natural laws that He has ordained.[113]

Your church's death has come about based on natural consequences God has ordained regarding the purpose of His church and the local life cycle He has put into place. While this reality is painful it is real. This is why I recommend Rainer's *Autopsy of a Deceased Church* to so many dying churches. Rainer masterfully lays out nine common mistakes (sins) that the local church commits which lead to the consequence of their death. Whether the church is willing to receive these truths or not, the consequences are real. We need to understand that God is not concerned with how we feel about His sovereignty, but He is concerned with our response to it.

Consider David's response to God's sovereign judgment over his sin with Bathsheba and Uriah. If you are unfamiliar with the story, turn to 2 Samuel 11-12 and reacquaint yourself. David's sin of adultery, and his act of murder to cover it up, leads to the death of an innocent child. When he is informed of God's sovereign decision, David seeks to change God's mind through prayer and fasting (2 Samuel 12:13-17). But God's sovereign choice had been made. David's response after the child dies puzzles his leaders and advisors. *"After the child dies, David resumes normal life. He has fully expressed his great grief. He has accepted the Lord's judgment."*[114]

---

[113] Ryrie, C. C. (1999). *Basic Theology: A Popular Systematic Guide to Understanding Biblical Truth* (pp. 48–49). Moody Press.

[114] Knowles, A. (2001). *The Bible guide* (1st Augsburg books ed., p. 144). Augsburg.

Certainly, there are times in God's sovereignty when He wishes for us to seek Him in prayer and to ask for what we perceive as a change of heart from God, but there are also times when God allows consequences to come into our lives based on His preordained will and sovereign structures. This aspect of God's sovereignty is not unique to David. Consider Aaron, God's chosen priest of Israel. Aaron's sons died when they disobeyed specific aspects of being ceremonially clean before approaching the holiness of God in their duties as priests. "Unfortunately, [Aaron's] sons Nadab and Abihu proved unworthy and were miraculously destroyed by fire. Aaron, though grief-stricken, accepted God's judgment (Lev. 10:3)." [115]

Notice that in both biblical examples, once God's sovereign plan was known, there was real grief but also a willingness to accept the hard truth of where the Lord was leading (ACCEPTANCE) and move forward with what God was doing. It is only when our church attenders and leaders can accept God's sovereignty that they can then see His hope which follows. I was recently humbled when I saw this same principle lived out in the life of a friend who decided to follow God's call to plant in a church.

Richard Pope, not only wrote the forward to this book, but he is a friend who has helped me see the sovereignty of God in a new and fresh light. Richard found out that his cancer had returned when he was about to plant Canvas Church in Salisbury, MD in 2020. What made the return of cancer most heinous was that it came with a terminal diagnosis. Richard, like any normal person given a terminal diagnosis, struggled with how to understand and accept God's sovereignty. To hear more about his journey, check out https://www.namb.net/send-network/resource/terminal-the-dying-church-planter/.

In this season, Richard sought out God's plan for hope through friends, colleagues, coaches, and the young, new disciples that the Lord had recently saved through this fledgling church plant. He confessed his real fears, concerns, and emotions while simultaneously processing God's sovereignty and timing. Where Richard landed is that God must have wanted him to plant a church while dealing with cancer. He

---

[115] Losch, R. R. (2008). In *All the People in the Bible: An A–Z Guide to the Saints, Scoundrels, and Other Characters in Scripture* (p. 2). William B. Eerdmans Publishing Company.

knows the Lord is capable of miraculous healing and that the Lord also may allow him to die. He is still unsure of the outcome, but he is certain that God will bring hope and victory if he is faithful to God's sovereign call.

Richard's planting journey was physically more difficult than any of us could have imagined. However, the miraculous, sovereign hand of God has sustained him and has blessed his obedience. Richard's church is growing exponentially with people's lives being saved, baptisms, and leadership development. They have even planted a new church 45 minutes northwest of their location in Cambridge, MD. His story is all about God's sovereignty and the willingness to receive what God is doing and to join Him where He is at work regardless of how we feel about it. Richard is living out what Henry Blackaby discovered in scripture:

> Too often, people assume that along with the role of leader comes the responsibility of determining what should be done. They develop aggressive goals. They dream grandiose dreams. They cast grand visions. Then they pray and ask God to join them in their agenda and to bless their efforts. That's not what spiritual leaders do. Spiritual leaders seek God's will, whether it is for their church or for their corporation, and then they marshal their people to pursue God's plan. [116]

When your people finally see that it is within God's sovereign plan for their church to die, then they will be able to accept the future hope that comes not from their will, but God's! Once they are grounded in God's sovereignty then they can receive the hope that only God can bring.

One of my favorite movies is *The Shawshank Redemption*. I think I have always been drawn to the movie because of how it brings out the best and worst of humanity. The main characters of the movie are Andy and Red. Andy is concerned that after Red is released from prison, he will give up hope. Therefore, Andy sends Red on a mysterious quest to find a buried and hidden box. In the box, Red finds money to help him join Andy and a letter where Andy reminds Red that "hope is a good thing, maybe the best of things, and no good thing ever dies. I will be hoping that this letter

---

[116] Blackaby, H., & Blackaby, R. (2001). *Spiritual Leadership: Moving People on to God's Agenda* (p. 23). B&H Publishing Group.

finds you and finds you well." [117] The letter breathes life into Red's hopeless reality. As the movie is closing Red contemplates:

> I find I'm so excited I can barely sit still or hold a thought in my head. I think it is the excitement only a free man can feel, a free man at the start of a long journey whose conclusion is uncertain. I hope I can make it across the border. I hope to see my friend, and shake his hand. I hope the Pacific is as blue as it has been in my dreams. **I hope**. [118]

As a leader, it is your primary task to instill and declare hope to the church that has accepted God's plan to allow them to die. "Because death is not an ultimate tragedy for Christians, their grief is without the sting experienced by those who have no hope."[119] So, don't shy away from confronting the truth of the situation while at the same time declaring and preaching the Gospel news grounded in a hopeful resurrection. While we know that our church is being led to death, we also know that "faith is the assurance of things hoped for, the conviction of things not seen." [120]

We may not know in what way God wants to resurrect His church, but what we do know is that He will bring goodness out of the grave. In this season, there will be those who will not want to accept, but if most of the church is prepared it is time to move forward. In Kübler-Ross' research, they found that conflicts "in regard to hope arose from two main sources. The first and most painful one was the conveyance of hopelessness either on part of the staff or family when the patient still needed hope. The second source of anguish came from the family's inability to accept

---

[117] Darabont, Frank (Director). 1995. *The Shawshank Redemption*. (2:15:16) Warner Bros. Entertainment Inc.

[118] Darabont, Frank (Director). 1995. *The Shawshank Redemption*. (2:17:08) Warner Bros. Entertainment Inc.

[119] Larsen, J. A. (1999). Grief. In D. G. Benner & P. C. Hill (Eds.), *Baker encyclopedia of psychology & counseling* (2nd ed., p. 520). Baker Books.

[120] *The Holy Bible: English Standard Version* (Heb 11:1). (2016). Crossway Bibles.

a patient's final stage". [121] It is your role to lead through acceptance to ensure that neither of these conflicts finds a footing in the church.

If your church is unable to arrive at this final phase, then death will come to the church in a more tragic form, but make no mistake: it *will* still come. While Kübler-Ross found that this situation was rare, I'm concerned that it exists at a higher probability within the church in America.

There are a few patients who fight to the end, who struggle [... and make] it almost impossible to reach this stage of acceptance. They are the ones who will say one day, "I just cannot make it anymore," the day they stop fighting, the fight is over. In other words, the harder they struggle to avoid the inevitable death, the more they try to deny it, the more difficult it will be for them to reach this final stage of acceptance with peace and dignity. [122]

This is why helping the church to come to acceptance is so important. What is at stake is what we talked about in Chapters 2 & 3: A grace-filled death versus a gut-wrenching one. One that is dignified versus one that lacks peace and dignity. I have stood beside the bed of both outcomes, as well as seen too often the parallel within the church. I pray often for churches and their leaders who are actively dying that they will choose the humble path of surrender and see a grace-filled death with a resurrection on the other side that is not of their making. Another reality that you will probably have to begin to introduce to the church is that death will mean a change in leadership.

Generally speaking, the leadership that leads the church to its death, is not the same leadership that will lead them out of the tomb. This is something that you will have to prepare your own heart for. If you are the existing pastor or the interim pastor, it is important that you prepare your church for the possibility of new leadership. This can be a shot to your ego as well as create some difficult decisions for the church leadership. But it is rare within a dying church that the seated pastor or the interim

[121] Kübler-Ross, Elisabeth. On Death and Dying: What the Dying Have to Teach Doctors, Nurses, Clergy and Their Own Families (p. 149). Scribner. Kindle Edition.

[122] Kübler-Ross, Elisabeth. On Death and Dying: What the Dying Have to Teach Doctors, Nurses, Clergy and Their Own Families (p. 125). Scribner. Kindle Edition.

pastor will be the one who will lead the church into the new vision of where God is calling. This reality is part of the acceptance phase of grief for the church and for you as the leader.

If you are looking for a Biblical example of this truth my editor, when reading this section, recalled David and Solomon with their unique roles in building the temple. David was instrumental in leading Israel to a time of peace, but to get there, he had to take the people through a difficult time of battle, and this required him to spill blood. However, Solomon came into leadership in a different time and era. He was poised to lead Israel through this next season and David had the humility to see this and receive this word from the Lord (See 1 Chronicles 22).

I'm not sure how many people have heard of a life-verse, but early in my Christian walk, I had friends who spoke of them. They communicated that some of us need a verse of scripture to shape our lives and remind us of certain truths that we need for our life-long journey as believers. This reality intrigued me, and in my quiet time, I reflected on my personal struggles and life. I discovered that I had deep-seated issues with pride. Pride manifested in the need to gain approval from others, the need to have my opinion validated, and how easily my self-esteem could be damaged by other leaders. So, I adopted James 4:6b early on as my life verse: "God opposes the proud but gives grace to the humble."[123]

I would come back to this passage often throughout my week and throughout my life. It grew into an eventual prayer that helped to cultivate humility within me. "Lord, where can I best serve you in this season that will expand your Kingdom?" This humble prayer has led me to and away from different ministry roles over the last 25 years. I place this reality before you now as a leader and as you consider "where the Lord is now leading you in this season?". God may be preparing a leader who is a better fit or has the right new vision for your dying church; if you do not prepare your people, or your own heart, for this possibility, then you might create a situation where your church is unable to receive the resurrection. Additionally, He is shaping you for a new role. God is sovereign, but in His sovereignty, He has chosen to look for and use humble, willing souls who will say YES to His will. "For the eyes

---

[123] *The Holy Bible: English Standard Version* (Jas 4:6). (2016). Crossway Bibles.

of the LORD run to and fro throughout the whole earth, to give strong support to those whose heart is blameless toward him." [124]

Be open to the reality that your role, or where you serve the Lord in this season, may need to change if God's new vision and plan for your church is to be received. You may stay at your current church but move into a pastoral care mode to serve the vision of the new pastor. It may be time for you to retire. You may need to move to a different church to take on a new interim role in helping a new church navigate its DEATH, BURIAL, and RESURRECTION. If this is hard for you, seek out a consultant or denominational leader and ask for an honest opinion. They may be able to help you see whether God has shaped your church for you to be the right leader or not in the next season.

May you and I have the humility "to number our days that we may get a heart of wisdom." [125] I know that God has not only numbered my days on this earth, but He has numbered my days as the current lead pastor of my church. He will one day call our church, and their current lead pastor, to die. As we embrace His call to lay down our lives before Him, I hope and pray that we will have the humility to receive what He is bringing us to and the courage to hand over control to Him once again. I pray that we might celebrate all that God has done and then rest awaiting His call to rise once again. That is the beauty of accepting His sovereign call to come and die.

---

[124] *The Holy Bible: English Standard Version* (2 Ch 16:9). (2016). Crossway Bibles.

[125] *The Holy Bible: English Standard Version* (Ps 90:12). (2016). Crossway Bibles.

## NEXT STEPS

1.  If you have not already read *Autopsy of a Deceased Church*, read it now and encourage your leadership and prayer team to get a copy and read it. Ask them as they read to accept with humility where God is leading the church in His sovereignty.

2.  If you are the pastor, begin to ask the Lord if you are the right person to lead the church in the next season. Open your life to other trusted people and ask your prayer team to pray over this with you. Journal your thoughts and concerns.

3.  Have an honest discussion with your leadership and prayer team as to how your church contributed to its death and decline based on what you read in *Autopsy of a Deceased Church*. Right these contributing issues into your journal for further prayer and reflection.

4.  Share how you believe the Lord has exposed how the current church has contributed to its death. Allow those issues to be expressed in repentant prayer before God within the public and private assembly of the church. Preach on the importance of having a repentant heart and accepting your role in the church's decline.

5.  Do not move forward if the bulk of the church has not arrived at acceptance and is repentant! If they are stuck, ask your prayer team why?

6.  If there are specific families stuck, confront them on why they are stuck. Be truthful and grace-filled in your response; however, also be ready to discipline a family who is unrepentant. Consider if the Lord is pruning His church so that it can move forward. You may have to ask the family to leave your fellowship if they are impeding the Lord's work. Remember there are blessed additions and subtractions to the body of Christ.

7.  As you sense the church accepting the situation, begin to turn the prayer life of the church to be thankful for the resurrection that the Lord is about to bring!

# 9

# The Funeral (A Celebration of Life)

*'Live in Christ, [die] in Christ, and the flesh need not fear death.'[126]*

*And we know that for those who love God all things work together for good, for those who are called according to his purpose.[127]*

Over the last few years, I have noticed that people are not having funerals. Several people within my congregation and the community in which I serve have opted for graveside services or no service at all. I even had a family member who died a few years ago who decided to have no service, be cremated, no obituary, and left no instructions as to how we should treat their remains. They were literally here one moment, and then in the next, there was no record of their passing or the celebration of their life. I do not bring up these observations because I am a morbid person, but because it indicates a shift in culture that is connected to how poorly we deal with death. In the recent past, death was thought of more as a part of life. In many cultures, there is a process for grieving/lamenting, and the funeral has been an important part of expressing our grief and support for the family.

In my own personal life, I have learned the importance of the local funeral service both as a pastor and as a fellow lamenter. At the time of writing this book, all my grandparents, parents and even one sibling have gone home to be with the Lord. A big part of dealing with the emotion of loss was the funeral service. In fact, the viewing was very unemotional for me, but the service tapped powerfully into my

---

[126] Water, M. (2002). *The Christian book of records* (p. 68). John Hunt Pub.

[127] *The Holy Bible: English Standard Version* (Ro 8:28). (2016). Crossway Bibles.

dealing with the deep feelings of hurt and loss. I have seen this reality also in the countless lives of families that I have served as a pastor as I led them through planning a funeral service to express their love and their sense of loss.

The funeral service is connected to helping the family and the congregation accept the reality of their situation. "One of the major goals of the funeral service is the facilitating of 'grief work.' The first segment of the grief journey is that of acceptance, facing up to the reality of death."[128] One of the reasons we tend to skip over this aspect of grief in modern times is we are attempting to avoid our grief. "Christian funeral rites are seen as instrumental for bereaved families to express their grief and accept their loss, and for friends to demonstrate their love and respect."[129] As a pastor, I take seriously my role to help the family to express their grief and loss through celebrating the life of the person that they love. If they choose not to have a service, then they miss out on a critical tool to help them deal with their grief.

Churches seem to have followed this trend of not having a final service or celebration when the final moment has come for a local gathering. In 2023, our church sent out a retired pastor about 45 minutes north of our gathering to assess and potentially lead a revitalization of a church that had been in decline for several years. In partnership with other churches and local associations, we agreed to support this pastor and his salary so that he would have an opportunity to assess where this local church was, and if there was the potential to bring health to the church.

During the year-long effort, the pastor worked with a handful of the remnant of this church to establish a school partnership, built community relationships with the fire department and other entities, led several prayer-walks where leaders and missionaries were able to engage with the local community, and built relationships through preaching and pastoring of the existing congregation. He quickly discovered that this church had a long season of being unhealthy and that they had little desire to turn their efforts outward to the community to reach those who don't

---

[128] Cadenhead, A., Jr. (1988). *Minister's manual for funerals* (p. 37). Broadman Press.

[129] Reid, D. G., Linder, R. D., Shelley, B. L., & Stout, H. S. (1990). In *Dictionary of Christianity in America*. InterVarsity Press.

know Jesus. Despite his leadership and efforts, the church continued to focus inward, and their only goal was to cling to life no matter what the cost. The interim pastor also began to discern that there was an unrepentant spirit of racism. On one of the prayer walks, conducted in partnership with several partnering churches, this issue was brought to the surface.

We met several people less than half a mile from this church who were of a different ethnic group than the local church being assessed. As we talked and prayed with them, we quickly learned that the church had a reputation in the community for racism and not creating a welcoming environment for other ethnic groups. The interim pastor communicated this issue to the church, who was in complete denial that this was a reality. Additionally, what he discerned was that their primary focus was to acquire a pastor to shepherd the existing few, and there was little heart to reach the people around the church: more specifically people from a different ethnic group.

Over the course of that year, he came to realize that this church was not going to turn the corner, and more than likely its lifecycle was ending. As this reality set in, he found himself in unfamiliar territory. One of the challenges was to understand that this was not a failure on his part, but merely the end of the life cycle of this local gathering.

The interim pastor and his wife did not think that they had the strength to lead the church through a closing. After all, all of his interim training was to either prepare the church for the next pastor or for a revitalization strategy to move forward. There was nothing in his training about how to close a church well. But what he had to do was gutsy and no other pastor who had previously been an interim had been honest enough about the church's unhealthiness and terminal trajectory. Eventually, once he and his wife got through the "what ifs", they were able to see what a privilege it would be to lead through this difficult season. An interesting dynamic was that the interim pastor and his wife also went through the stages of grief themselves while having to lead the church toward acceptance of the terminal diagnosis.

Once they processed and prayed through this reality, the interim pastor scheduled a business meeting at the church to explain where the church was after one year and reminded them of all the efforts that had been attempted toward revitalization. He came to me before the meeting and asked, "what should I do?" I advised "If the church is dead, it is appropriate to have a funeral and to celebrate what God had done in the life of the church".

At the business meeting, the interim used no notes and talked about the history of the church and the different seasons the church had experienced. He shared his conviction that the church had come to the end of its life cycle. The interim pastor shared from his heart, for he had grown to love the remnant that was left in this church and believed that they deserved to hear the truth from a compassionate pastor who had been leading through these final stages of grief. He reminded the remaining nine attenders that the church is not a building, but a people who gather around a confession of who Jesus is and are energized by His mission. Eventually, he let them know that he believed it was time to close the church. He then proposed a Celebration of Life to celebrate all the things that God had done over the last 136 years. The church had arrived at the final stage of acceptance and received what he had to share, even though it was a difficult message. They scheduled the final date for their final service.

The interim pastor went through old photos, documents, and stories with his congregation and used all that info to put together a presentation for celebrating the life of the church. There were documents showing people who had been married and baptized going all the way back to 1886. In many ways, this process reminded me of when a family comes in to prepare for the funeral of a loved one and they bring photos and memorabilia. Grieving families share special stories with their pastor that they would like to see shared at the service and they offer special songs or elements for the service that they believe would honor their loved one and their loved one's Savior! This same process unfolded for the collective life of this church.

The church posted on their Facebook a celebration of life and they got some interesting comments. Many of the posts were from people who had attended in the past and were grieving the death of the church's closing. Some people or organizations sought to profit from the church's death and offered to buy the church and property for a quick and easy profit. Ironically, many of those who had grown up at the church did not return when revitalization efforts took place, but they did return for the celebration of life or expressed their condolences. Many of those previous attenders had decided to go to churches within 20 to 30 minutes of the church that they had grown up in. The interim pastor believed that the sin of racism was the reason that these previous families did not return. The remnant families certainly did not hate people of a different race, but their upbringing and racial bias came through in their language, comments, their temperament and in the way that they were unable to create a welcoming environment for the surrounding community.

At their last service, there was a large gathering. There were people there who had grown up going to the church, the remnant that had stayed, and the interim pastor and his family. Surprisingly, the atmosphere was not one of sorrow but one of celebration. Baptisms were remembered, weddings, special services, and even ministries of the youth and children, who had impacted many in the community in the past years. The overall atmosphere was one of celebration of all that God had done and how much it was a privilege to be a part of what had happened. In many ways, it reminded the interim of how different a Christian funeral is from a secular one. God's people grieve with hope and remembrance, not mere finality, and despair.

Once the service was done, the interim followed up over the next few days and weeks with the congregants recommending good Bible-preaching churches that were within 15-30 minutes of the old church. Partnering churches continued their support to prepare the property and maintain it for the older congregants. The interim continued to help the church grieve as well as work on estate planning and administrative elements of transition. The church leadership decided they would prefer to sell the church to another church and give the money to local church plants that were advancing the Kingdom of Christ in their area. This was the first sign of new life and resurrection. But there were more signs of life and resurrection to follow based on the church's courage to embrace the death and burial of their own church.

One of the remnant families had children who were part of a church plant that did not have a building but were doing great Kingdom work. Once the church plant found out that the church was closing, they contacted the church leadership about obtaining or purchasing the property. Ironically, the church plant is predominantly from the ethnic group that had felt unconnected to the current local gathering. At this time of the writing of this book, the church plant is working with current church leadership, a bank, and a real estate agent to acquire the property to begin a new season of ministry in that community. If everything pans out, then God will have brought about a resurrection from the death of this church which may reach every ethnic group in the community while healing the past racism in a way that will ultimately bring the Lord the glory through the death, burial, and resurrection of His Church.

While this church's death was physical in nature, and the funeral was literally a celebration of life, not all funerals of a church are literal. Many times, the funeral is a recognition of grieving what was so that the church can embrace the possibility of what can be. However, before expounding more on those processes I would like to recognize and offer some wisdom from Tom Rainer about how a church can physically die well. Rainer suggests "four ways [...] a church [can die] with dignity."
[130]

1.  *Sell the property and give the funds to another church, perhaps a new church that has begun or will soon begin.*

2.  *Give the building to another church.*

3.  *If your church is in a transitional neighborhood, turn over the leadership and property to those who actually reside in the neighborhood.*

4.  *Merge with another church, but let the other church have the ownership and leadership of your church.* [131]

With each of Rainer's suggestions for dying well, a church needs to exercise a humble prayerful approach seeking to discover what God wants to do with His church. After all, humility is a required facet for any growth or resurrection to take place. It was humility that led Jesus to His death, and it was the apostle Paul who commended

---

[130] Rainer, Thom S.. Autopsy of a Deceased Church: 12 Ways to Keep Yours Alive (Location: 821). B&H Publishing Group. Kindle Edition.

[131] Rainer, Thom S.. Autopsy of a Deceased Church: 12 Ways to Keep Yours Alive (Location: 856). B&H Publishing Group. Kindle Edition.

this attitude as a necessary element to growth (Phil 2:1-11). As I shared in the chapter, "A Grace Filled Death", a humble prayer life prepares the soil of God's church to embrace the death of what was so that the possibility of what can be can be raised to life. While not all deaths are physical for a revitalization, they all follow the same precepts involving humble prayer, repentance, and acceptance.

Many times, the church must embrace the death of previous culture, process, leadership paradigm, or tradition. For instance, when I first arrived at a local church, they were singing hymns and 80's style praise choruses. A lot of the worship style was developed from denominational norms and the current aging congregants (average age was 75 when I arrived). It would have been a mistake to think that the style of worship was the issue or any aspect of the worship liturgy. In fact, I only made a few changes to worship to be able to reach a larger audience and improve the overall quality. As the church grew, and we started to reach more musicians and artists, they brought with them new perspectives and challenges to our culture of worship. Our worship team had to go through a mini death within the church to embrace these new attenders who wanted to use their gifts. Both the old guard and the new attenders had to embrace the Christ-like humility described in Philippians 2 and prayerfully discover how the church would express a new form of worship. It may surprise you that the changes were not stylistic as much as they were helping the old and new attenders to embrace the crucified life: DEATH, BURIAL, and RESURRECTION. The death did not come easy and at times it was scary and fun to watch.

At one particular worship practice our new worship director (Kevin Les Callette) let our organist (Jane Locke) know that we needed to make a change in the flow of service. The change was logical and based on what we wanted to accomplish with the message that week. It involved our organist (Jane), of more than 50 years, to accept a change in what instrument they would be playing. Kevin asked that she remain on keys and not transition to the organ. Kevin was in his 50's and the organist was in her 80's at the time.

The organist reminded our new worship leader that she could play the keyboard sound he wanted from the organ. But he was more concerned about the length of time and break in service to transition to the organ. He did not have anything against the church organ, he just wanted to create a certain moment and knew that a long break in the service would not be conducive. I could have stepped in to resolve the argument, but I felt that I also needed to let each of them work it out. They had some direct words with one another, and Jane reluctantly agreed to play from the keys and not walk across the entire sanctuary to the organ. However, she also reached around and cranked up the amp behind the keyboard she was playing. When Kevin went to count in the song, she found the loudest organ sound she could find on the keyboard with the amp cranked all the way up and blasted us all off the stage! I laughed inside as Kevin ducked his head and turned red. While I look back on the situation with humor and nostalgia today, I can also see three areas where we violated the principle of humility within Philippians 2.

I was the one that suggested the flow change and I asked Kevin to lead through it. I really set him up to fail and springing it on Jane was unfair. Jane really showed a lack of humility and aggression that surprised me for her maturity. But, all us can regress when certain buttons get pushed. We later learned this woman was a fiery passionate lady who was in better shape than both of us in her 80's. Not that the situation came close to blows, but if it had she could have taken us both! Lastly our worship leader tried through the force of will and personality to make it happen. When we stepped back from the situation and prayed about it, we knew what to do.

We learned that Jane had a love for pie. So, the three of us went out for pie later that week and talked through the changes that were being proposed. When we sat down, we prayed and talked about the "why" behind certain proposed changes. All three of us made some compromises and died some to self and what arose from the situation was better than what we had planned for the next season of ministry. This became a pattern for our team for a few years: Every time we sensed it was time to make a change, we made an appointment for pie. Jane was an intelligent woman; I'm sure she figured out the pattern quickly. I often wonder if it changed her love for pie over time, but I saw no evidence of that reality. At each pie encounter, we all died some, to discover how Christ might live in a new worship reality. Jane is now with the Lord. Our worship leader and I miss having pie and talking about changes in worship. While I look forward most to celebrating the Lord's table in heaven, I also look forward to catching up over pie with Jane. Who knows, she may have some heavenly changes in worship that she can catch me up on as I enter eternal worship with her.

Over the course of 8 years with this church, worship styles have changed consistently. It does not match a specific genre but is a larger reflection of the diversity of our church. There are banjo players, guitar players, keyboard players, traditionalists, contemporary artists, and even heavy metal with bluegrass aficionados. The worship ministry has created a great example of how DEATH, BURIAL, and RESURRECTION happen all the time as the church advances and grows.

At each juncture of change, there was an eclectic celebration (a funeral) producing a new hope and beautiful, fresh, resurrected life. This pattern continues to impact areas like Sunday school, small groups, ministries, outreach, and even preaching styles. I think embracing and celebrating the process of something dying so that something new can live is one of the healthy realities of a church that has learned to embrace the change process. After all, the only constant in a changing universe is change!

## NEXT STEPS

1.  As you meet with your prayer team and leadership, ask if there is any area of church tradition or programming that you need to have a funeral service. What form should it take to celebrate its impact on the Kingdom and the local church?

2.  Has your church come to a complete DEATH of the local gathering like the church mentioned in this chapter? If so, do you need to plan a final service to celebrate the church's life and impact on the advancement of the Kingdom?

3.  Remember, if you stop having public services, it does not mean that you can't meet for Bible Study and prayer as you begin to prepare your heart for the rebirth that God is about to bring. Be creative as you consider how to celebrate the DEATH of one season so that you can prepare the church for the BIRTH of a new one.

4.  Come back to that question about who the next pastor should be. Have you heard from the Lord clearly if your current pastor or a different pastor will be the one to lead through the next season? If you have heard, make sure that you honor an existing pastor both financially and by honoring their years of good service!

5.  Don't hesitate to reach out to consultants, other churches, or denominational leaders for help in this season.

6.  Update your journal.

# 10

# The Resurrection

*[25] Jesus said to her, "I am the resurrection and the life. Whoever believes in me, though he die, yet shall he live, [26] and everyone who lives and believes in me shall never die. Do you believe this?" [132]*

*"Only where graves are is there resurrection." We practice our death by giving up our will to live on our own terms. Only in that relinquishment or renunciation are we able to practice resurrection. [133]*

For the last few chapters, we have weathered the phases of grief by staying focused on the power of hope! Hope is anchored axiomatically to the resurrection of Christ. The resurrection is the greatest miracle of human history. Paul when describing it to the Corinthian Church said, "[3] For I delivered to you as of first importance what I also received: that Christ died for our sins in accordance with the Scriptures, [4] that he was buried, that he was raised on the third day in accordance with the Scriptures" [134] It is at this point in our journey together, we have to part ways with Elisabeth Kübler-Ross' research.

While she was able to help us navigate the phases of grief, she is of little help when it comes to understanding the resurrections' importance for the life cycle of the local church. However, if we have truly died as a church then we need to understand that the resurrection that is taking place is not one of our own making, but of God's.

---

[132] *The Holy Bible: English Standard Version* (Jn 11:25–26). (2016). Crossway Bibles.

[133] Peterson, Eugene H.. The Pastor: A Memoir (p. 290). HarperCollins. Kindle Edition.

[134] *The Holy Bible: English Standard Version* (1 Co 15:3–4). (2016). Crossway Bibles.

This reliance on God to bring the resurrection is of critical importance if we are to see a church rebirthed that is not of our will, but completely of His. While this reality may be self-apparent to many, it is not always plain to Americans who tend to rely too much on their own ingenuity, creativity, and hard work ethic.

Mark Clifton, like many church leaders, considered this reality when he was considering revitalization juxtaposition with church planting.

> Like most of my church planter friends, I figured it was easier to start a new church in a school down the street than to resurrect a dying one. And honestly, I was right. In my experience, it is easier to start a new church than to resurrect a dying one. Then again, what's right and what's expedient are rarely the same in Jesus' economy. [135]

As you begin to ponder and pray about what God is about to do to resurrect your church, keep in mind that His miracle will be unique and ultimately it will bring glory to him and not you or your church. You will need "wisdom for your journey and a renewed hope that the God who sent his Son to die for the church longs to resurrect declining congregations throughout North America and the world. [136] But His desire to raise up a dead church is connected to His power and now ours. One of the problems in American Christianity is how much our culture has conditioned us to think that everything is about us.

I received Christ's saving power in my life when I was 17 years of age, but by 19 I had fallen away. There are a lot of reasons for this falling away season, but ultimately it was because I decided to make my faith about me, and not about what the Lord wanted to do in me and through me. A book that was instrumental in my return to the faith as well as to better understand my Christian purpose was Rick Warren's *Purpose Driven Life*. At the very onset of the book, he reminds his readers

---

[135] Clifton, Mark. Reclaiming Glory: Creating a Gospel Legacy throughout North America (p. 9). B&H Publishing Group. Kindle Edition.

[136] Clifton, Mark. Reclaiming Glory: Creating a Gospel Legacy throughout North America (p. 78). B&H Publishing Group. Kindle Edition.

that "IT'S NOT ABOUT YOU". [137]As I read the book with my wife and church, I had some hard moments of confession and self-examination.

I began to understand that the resurrection of Christ was not just for me and my salvation but was also for my family and community. I remember a particularly difficult evening when my wife and I were on Day 20 in the book. Day twenty's title is "Restoring Broken Fellowship" and as we read that day's devotion, I realized our marriage needed to be resurrected. [138] Worse yet, I realized that for our marriage to be resurrected, I needed to confess to my wife that I had not been completely faithful to her while I was in the US Navy. It would have been my preference to just leave my indiscretion in the past and move forward by loving her completely now, but that would not have been a sincere and honest way to move forward. I think my reservation to be confessional with my wife was connected to my fear that she would leave me as a result.

She certainly would have grounds to: this was one of the areas that the Bible gave justifiable grounds for divorce, and I wanted to save my marriage not destroy it through confession. In the devotion, I was confronted with Warren's admonition: "If you are serious about restoring a relationship, you should begin with admitting your own mistakes or sin." [139] I was serious about restoring my marriage, and I could sense that this area of my sin was causing a separation between God, my wife, and me. (That's what sin does after all). As I prayed more about it, I knew I needed to be confessional with my wife and I would have to let God bring a miracle into our lives that would overcome my sin.

So, the evening after our devotion I sat her down and confessed. As part of my confession, I told my wife that I dearly loved her and I was not confessing to hurt her, but to be honest and transparent with her. I shared that I believed for our

---

137 Warren, Rick. The Purpose Driven Life: What on Earth Am I Here For? (p. 21). Zondervan. Kindle Edition.

138 Warren, Rick. The Purpose Driven Life: What on Earth Am I Here For? (p. 152). Zondervan. Kindle Edition.

139 Warren, Rick. The Purpose Driven Life: What on Earth Am I Here For? (p. 157). Zondervan. Kindle Edition.

marriage to be on good footing, I needed her forgiveness and that I wanted to be and become the husband that God was calling me to be and the one she deserved. I waited for the fallout and was ready to accept whatever consequences may have come from my confession.

She not only forgave me but was confessional about her failures at times and her desire for our marriage to be saved and resurrected. We cried a lot that night, prayed a lot and the Lord resurrected our marriage in a way that was not of our making but His! To this day I still feel the remorse of my failure, but alongside of it I also feel blessed beyond my understanding with a gracious wife who was able to forgive because she is first in love with a gracious Savior who is in the business of resurrecting the dead.

As an aside, it pierces my heart to hear couples say that they could never forgive their husband or wife if they cheated on them. I certainly have no grounds to judge those who would pursue a divorce out of infidelity, but I also know that our Lord is able to save any marriage if both parties are willing to be honest, confessional, and surrender to God's path toward reconciliation/resurrection. At the time of my confession, we had been married for 8 years. At the time of the writing of this book, we have been married for 32 years! If God had not resurrected my marriage, I do not know where I would be or if I would have followed Him into pastoral ministry. We would not have had any children, our understanding of God's grace and power would have been diminished, and we would have allowed Satan to deliver a final blow to what God had put together.

Just like God resurrected my marriage, He wants to resurrect your church. It is not for you alone, but for all those who will one day benefit from that resurrection. Because our marriage was saved, we have a marital union that has been forged together in a way that is now truly inseparable. We have children who know what unconditional love is. We have a church family who receives the grace of Christ easily from us because of how much His grace changed us. He wants that same thing in your church. But, the great danger is that you will either give up or manufacture a resurrection of human hands.

Maybe you fear confronting the hard truths of how you and the congregation have sinned and fallen short. I know that I did not want to be real about my failure within my marriage. Churches fail to receive God's resurrection because they are unable to be truly vulnerable, humble, and repentant. People, and the churches they occupy, are too concerned with hiding their sin instead of revealing it. But as many of you know, the beginning of healing is revealing!

If you sense that your church and its leadership have not been transparent, take another look at the common things that brought death to the local church detailed within Rainer's *Autopsy of a Deceased Church*. Did your church have a moment of confession that matched some of the common areas of sin that Rainer brings up? Every church I've seen resurrected had this moment of repentance and confession. If your church has not had it, more than likely a miraculous resurrection is not coming your way. Instead, you are headed for some sort of pain or spiritual divorce that will bring greater pain.

The other result of my marriage being resurrected was the collateral blessing. As a result of my repentance and my wife's forgiveness, our family has been blessed generationally. Our children grew up in a home that would have been radically different had I not been real and confessional with my wife. The same thing is true of your church. When God brings a resurrection, it is not for you and your church alone. The community, society, and the Kingdom will all benefit when a church is resurrected based on God's making.

Mark Clifton shared this about the resurrection of one of the churches he was honored to lead through revitalization: "Our neighborhood was noticeably better because God had resurrected a declining Wornall Road Baptist." [140] Notice that the benefit of the church's resurrection was that their community was made better because the grace of Christ was resurrected within that local church that shared it with their neighbors, family and community. As you pray in expectation of God's miraculous resurrection for your church, be ready for Him to challenge you to sacrifice your comfort.

---

[140] Clifton, Mark. Reclaiming Glory: Creating a Gospel Legacy throughout North America (p. 94). B&H Publishing Group. Kindle Edition.

Remember that the Apostle Paul pursued Christ to "know him and the power of his resurrection, and may share his sufferings, becoming like him in his death, **11** that by any means possible I may attain the resurrection from the dead. [141]

When my current church experienced resurrection there were leadership changes, programmatic changes, and polity changes. Some of those changes were spoken of in Chapter 2: A Grace-filled Death. However, there is a specific story with the former youth director leader that comes to mind when we think about the miraculous nature of a sustainable, Divine church resurrection. As I have shared before, revitalization is not about small changes or tweaks but radical rebirth.

We were about a year into our church's resurrection and Scott Paulson (our former youth director) came to me and said he wanted to chat. You should know that Scott kept the youth ministry alive when no one else was able or willing to make an investment. He many times sustained the ministry as an outreach to the community even when the church was unable to financially support this ministry. Often, he paid for the program out of his pocket, so when he came to me and said that he wanted to talk, HE HAD MY EAR. Scott said that he recently had made two observations that he just wanted to bring to my attention.

He was doing the church attendance count one Sunday morning when he noticed that "there were more of them than there were of us". What he meant was that there were so many new members who had come to Christ and been baptized over the last year that they outnumbered the remnant that had been there for the last 20 years. He went on to say that he was impressed with all of the changes and how the church had weathered them. Then he paused, I think weighing his next thought against injuring my ego and leadership. He said that if two particular people were still alive and active in the church, none of the changes connected with the rebirth of our church would have taken place. He was careful to offer that he made this observation not to diminish my leadership, but just simply as a fact.

The particular people in question had hindered his former efforts to reach students across the street because the students did not fit within the demographic that those people thought would make up a church of noble character. Additionally, Scott told

---

[141] *The Holy Bible: English Standard Version* (Php 3:10–11). (2016). Crossway Bibles.

me that this specific group of people had been opposed to any kind of change for his entire tenure while he was at the church. The former pastor and his family had tried to implement change, but were thwarted often by this same group of people.

The former pastor visited our church with his family the summer after we had begun to lead radical change in the church to support God's new vision. The former pastor and his family told me on more than one occasion during their visit that they were so happy and delighted to see what God was doing. They had been praying for similar changes for many years while they were there. Their humility and encouragement had a deep impact on me and encouraged me regarding the season we were now enjoying.

As I reflected more on Scott's observations, I confirmed he was probably correct, and I told him so. What he was discovering was that there was a miraculous move of the hand of God, as well as the Lord's perfect timing, that were key factors in the church's resurrection. While this is humbling, it is also encouraging. It reminded me that the Lord had brought about our rebirth not by my leadership, ingenuity, or creativity but by His powerful hand based on our response to His leading us into DEATH, BURIAL, AND RESURRECTION.

Ultimately, what I want you and your team to understand is that resurrection comes by the Lord's hand and is based on His chosen form. One of the realities that our church leadership was considering before my arrival was turning the church building and all assets over to a church planter who would replant our church. This would have involved the church completely shutting down Sunday services and all discipleship programming, and then rebirthing as a new church once the new church planting team had been assembled and was ready to launch. While this is not ultimately what God called our church toward, they were ready to respond however our Lord called them from the tomb.

As you prayerfully consider how God is specifically calling your church to rise, let me offer again the most common forms of resurrection that Tom Rainer's research found to be effective:

1. *Sell the property and give the funds to another church, perhaps a new church that has begun or will soon begin.*

2. *Give the building to another church.*

3. *If your church is in a transitional neighborhood, turn over the leadership and property to those who actually reside in the neighborhood.*

4. *Merge with another church, but let the other church have the ownership and leadership of your church.* [142]

Below I offer some other options I have seen in my tenure as a leader within the revitalization realm:

5. Prayerfully bring on a new leadership team and pastor who will restart the church. The pastor should have experience in former works of revitalization or have been specifically trained for this effort.

6. Work with your denomination or a church planting network to re-plant the church with an intentional replant team.

7. Start a second service with a local church planter who can use the facility to reach the community. This can later turn into a merger.

8. Liquidate all assets of the church and invest them into other church plants or missions that are advancing the Gospel.

9. Other! I have learned that our Lord is creative, and He can bring all kinds of options when He arrives at our door and knocks. If you sense that He has brought a unique option, seek out an experienced consultant to advise you on that unique possibility to ensure it is not of your making but is from God's hand. We all need to be careful that we do not deceive ourselves.

---

[142] Rainer, Thom S.. Autopsy of a Deceased Church: 12 Ways to Keep Yours Alive (Location: 856). B&H Publishing Group. Kindle Edition.

One thing is for sure: whatever option our God brings will require humility to receive. A book that has been helpful in my formation to better understand the pastor role is Eugene Peterson's *The Pastor.*

In the book, he talks about the planting of his church and Belair, Md. A particularly touching part of the book for me was Eugene's interaction with a church that had recently died. Eugene shared that "Two months before our arrival, the Sparrow's Point Presbyterian Church, twenty miles south of us, had closed its doors for good." [143] The pastor of the church offered Eugene several items used in their weekly worship to help with his church plant: "a communion table, a baptismal font, three large pulpit chairs—all made of oak—and a set of communion ware complete with chalice, paten, and linen." [144]

As the pastor of the dying church offered these items, Eugene could sense "It was an emotional transaction [… and] realized what he was feeling, the loss of the symbols that had defined and centered his work for twenty-five years". [145] Try and absorb the emotion as well as the transactional investment in new life from death:

> He reminisced over his life with this congregation and welcomed me as I received what was left of it in the table and font and pulpit chairs. Conversation smoothed the transition. I thanked him for entrusting me with these holy things that would also define and center my work. He blessed me as I prepared to develop this new church. [146]

While we might grieve the passing of the former church, in our biblical acceptance that death proceeds resurrection we see how the Lord invested in the birth of a new church through the humility of the former pastor that would build upon the foundation of the dying church to reach more people to expand the Kingdom. This is the kind of humility that makes a way where our Lord can bring life out of death.

---

[143] Peterson, Eugene H.. The Pastor: A Memoir (p. 109). HarperCollins. Kindle Edition.

[144] Peterson, Eugene H.. The Pastor: A Memoir (p. 109). HarperCollins. Kindle Edition.

[145] Peterson, Eugene H.. The Pastor: A Memoir (p. 109). HarperCollins. Kindle Edition.

[146] Peterson, Eugene H.. The Pastor: A Memoir (p. 109). HarperCollins. Kindle Edition.

The question for you and your leadership team is: will you accept the kind of resurrection the Lord is envisioning, or will you cling only to ones that are palpable for your current gathering? I have worked with almost 100 churches to date on revitalization. There have only been a handful that have seen a physical resurrection: the ones that have prayerfully submitted to whatever the Lord wanted to do to expand His Kingdom. The churches that experienced an awful death stayed centered on saving their building or gathering instead of dying to self. In the end, every church experienced death and acceptance. The defining difference in their acceptance was connected to their humility.

As you pray with your church toward the form of acceptance that will come your way, meditate on the Apostle Paul's words on humility that he offered to the church in Philippi:

> [1] So if there is any encouragement in Christ, any comfort from love, any participation in the Spirit, any affection and sympathy, [2] complete my joy by being of the same mind, having the same love, being in full accord and of one mind. [3] Do nothing from selfish ambition or conceit, but in humility count others more significant than yourselves. [4] Let each of you look not only to his own interests, but also to the interests of others. [5] Have this mind among yourselves, which is yours in Christ Jesus, [6] who, though he was in the form of God, did not count equality with God a thing to be grasped, [7] but emptied himself, by taking the form of a servant, being born in the likeness of men. [8] And being found in human form, he humbled himself by becoming obedient to the point of death, even death on a cross.[147]

May you and I humbly accept whatever form the Lord leads our church in for our DEATH, BURIAL, and RESURRECTION! Furthermore, may it not just make Paul's joy complete but our Savior's as we value His Kingdom above ours. May God's Spirit bring humility to all of us as we seek to honor His call to rise and receive His resurrection!

---

[147] *The Holy Bible: English Standard Version* (Php 2:1–8). (2016). Crossway Bibles.

## NEXT STEPS

1. Review your journal and ensure that you see specific places where your church has expressed repentance for its role in the decline of God's Church. Ask your prayer team and leadership for specific examples.

2. If there is still a lack of public repentance, ask your prayer team and your leadership team for insight. Discuss how specific confrontations and disciplinary situations are going. Address specific areas brought up. If you are stuck, ask what phase of grief you may still be in and restudy that part of this book and patiently move forward.

3. Review with your prayer and leadership team the 9 common forms of resurrection listed in this chapter. Do you have a sense of which one, a combination of which ones, or a unique way that the Lord is calling your church toward resurrection? Ensure that both your prayer and leadership team are in alignment. If they are not, have them meet, pray, and work together until they reach unity. This may take more than one meeting, so be patient.

4. Communicate the vision of how you believe the Lord is calling your church toward resurrection to the congregation. Allow for feedback and address concerns with the HOPE that God has guided your team toward. Be willing to adjust, but do not surrender the overarching vision. Remember, GOD IS BRINING A RESURRECTION!

5. Strategize with the leadership team, and potentially a denominational or external consultant, as to what changes would need to be made to support the Resurrected Vision the church has received.

6. If you are the interim or seated pastor, ask your prayer team, leadership team, and family if you are the right pastor to lead all the changes required to see the church support the resurrection that God is bringing. Have the humility to step down or step forward based on the feedback you receive.

7. If your pastor steps down, honor their service and commitment to the church. Both finically and with a form of celebration for their ministry. Appoint new interim leaders where needed. Begin a new search for the

pastor, or leader, being called to lead the church through the RESURRECTION GOD has called you toward.

8. Continue to meet as a prayer team and appoint a new leader if necessary.

# 11

# Living the Resurrected Life

*[37] And no one puts new wine into old wineskins. If he does, the new wine will burst the skins and it will be spilled, and the skins will be destroyed. [38] But new wine must be put into fresh wineskins. [39] And no one after drinking old wine desires new, for he says, 'The old is good.'* [148]

*It may be hard for an egg to turn into a bird: it would be a jolly sight harder for it to learn to fly while remaining an egg.* [149]

Once you know that you have turned the corner, God has provided a pathway forward to a resurrection and momentum is on your side, you are ready to lead major change. The key here is that God has made evident the pathway forward and now you and the leadership team will have to adjust the church to walk within that new resurrected reality. You must prepare and structure your systems, processes, and leadership to support the new vision. The new vision will require continual leadership and maintenance. But make no mistake: the lead/senior pastor is the vision carrier at this point of the resurrected direction of the church.

If you have retained the same lead pastor, it is important that a new group of people be added to the leadership circle to ensure that a fresh leadership lens is brought to the change process. If you have brought on a new leader at this point, you need to ensure that their new team has some stability by having people from the previous leadership ethos who share the new vision and are able to submit to what God is

---

[148] *The Holy Bible: English Standard Version* (Lk 5:37–39). (2016). Crossway Bibles.

[149] Lewis, C. S.. Mere Christianity (C.S. Lewis Signature Classics) (p. 198). HarperCollins. Kindle Edition.

doing. It is also possible to have the previous pastor have a new role in the church at this point with pastoral care or helping to manage the church, providing that the previous pastor can humbly submit to the new vision and leadership of the new team. This can be tricky, but with continued prayer and guileless conversations, the possibilities for the new team are boundless.

One of the greatest dangers within the church is what happens in the mindset of the congregation post-resurrection. It is easy to behold the miracle of salvation/resurrection and then miss the reality that major change is coming to support the new resurrected life. It is common for people to be excited initially about the new direction of the church but miss that you are headed toward an entirely new ball game. This is the danger that we must avoid in post-resurrection living.

This danger is not limited to the church: this danger lives in the cognitive dissonance between leadership and management. "Management is about seeking order and stability; leadership is about seeking adaptive and constructive change." [150] Peter Drucker put it this way, "Management is doing things right; Leadership is doing the right thing". Leaders, by their very nature, embrace and move toward change like a moth drawn to a flame. Managers conversely seek to maintain order and the status quo like a tortoise who is moving steadily toward an objective. While it is true that you need both managers and leaders to be a successful and balanced organization, you also need to properly place them within their proper roles. Additionally, you must share a compelling and detailed vision that equips both your leaders and your managers to use their unique gifting in harmony to undergird the newly resurrected church.

Once my church had experienced resurrection, you could sense momentum shifting. The resurrection that was brought to Grace was one of supplying a new pastor, with a new vision to reach the community, by creating a new type of team made up of both existing and new leaders. Once Christ declared that resurrection to the remnant leadership it was time to reframe, lead and reorganize our church so it could support that new vision. Otherwise, momentum would have been short-lived if our team had

---

[150] Northouse, Peter G.. Leadership: Theory and Practice (Location: 606). SAGE Publications. Kindle Edition.

not continued to lead through change. What I want to do in this chapter is introduce you to Change Management, offer you our simple 4-step process to navigate change, and contextualize that change process enabling you and your team to properly navigate the dichotomy between managers and leaders.

Earlier in the book, I offered that the leaders in church revitalization said to grab all that you can on Change Management. Ironically, that is because most pastors are not taught anything regarding the subject in Bible College or Seminary. I have used the LOGOS Bible software for more than 20 years and have built my theological library over that span of time. I began using the software when attending Bible College. When I did a search for the topic of "Change Management" I got one hit, which was a reference with no major content, out of 2,425 source books and documents! So, I'm assuming that most people reading this book have not been exposed to Change Management. However, if you have or have someone on your team that understands this process you are blessed.

"Organizational change management is the process of guiding organizational change to a successful resolution, and it typically includes three major phases: preparation, implementation, and follow-through." [151] In 2011 if you searched Amazon "books on 'change and management' [it] turned up 6,153 titles, each with a distinct take on the topic." [152] The same search in 2023 returned over 20,000 titles! The amount of material on this topic continues to expand in every field where change is needed, but the church is lagging.

With such a large body of research now available, I offer the following suggestions to help you and your leadership team parse through so that you can get to application expeditiously. If you or anyone on your team has experience with Change Management you would be wise to use their background, research, and process. Good leaders know that effectiveness trumps creativity all day long.

---

[151] Stobierski, T. (2020, January 21). ORGANIZATIONAL CHANGE MANAGEMENT: WHAT IT IS & WHY IT'S IMPORTANT. Harvard Business School Online. (https://online.hbs.edu/blog/post/organizational-change-management).

[152] Harvard Business Review. HBR's 10 Must Reads on Change Management (Location 2549). Perseus Books Group. Kindle Edition.

Therefore, if you or your team has a background in Change Process then leverage what you know and build upon it.

This could be a denominational leader, a businessperson who has led a change process, or another pastor who has led a change process who has time to coach you and your team. Again, it is better to build on available relationships and wisdom for leading change than trying to invent a whole new process on your own. If you do not have access to someone on your team or in your network, then I offer the process that I used for our church in 2015 and continue to use to lead new change processes.

When I was working on my *MA in Ethical Leadership*, I was prescribed several books to read that were helpful in developing my understanding of Change Management:

- Chaleff, I. (2009). *The courageous follower*. (Third Edition). San Francisco: Berret-Koehler Publishers, Inc. ISBN 978-1605092737

- Harvard Business Review. (2011). *On change management*. Boston, MA: Harvard Business Review Press. ISBN 978-1422158005

- Myerson, D. E. (2008). *Rocking the boat: How to effect change without making trouble*. ISBN 978-1422121382

All of these are great resources, but Harvard Business Review's book on Change Management was the most useful and resourceful book on practically leading change. It not only helps you understand the general theory but provides multiple examples of actual change processes. I was able to draw from the process in a few ways: it confirmed the previous two revitalizations I had been a part of, and I saw the principles mirrored in the senior leadership from both of those churches. I was able to translate my prior two experiences practically into the changes I led our current church through.

More specifically, one of the examples within the book was a non-profit hospital (Beth Israel Deaconess Medical Center) that I thought closely resembled the local church in structure and purpose. From this example, I adapted a 4-step process that is easy to understand and manage as a leader for the local church. Before I present the sequential process, look at the importance of first understanding who your leaders and managers are within your church:

FACED WITH THE NEED for massive change, most managers respond predictably. They revamp the organization's strategy, then round up the usual set of suspects—people, pay, and processes—shifting around staff, realigning incentives, and rooting out inefficiencies. They then wait patiently for performance to improve, only to be bitterly disappointed. For some reason, the right things still don't happen. [153]

When you look at what managers add: organizational strategy, human resources, processes, aligned incentives and rooting out inefficiencies; they are all needed and very important dimensions for organizational success. However, a well-oiled machine traveling in the wrong direction will still arrive at the wrong destination. It has been my experience that many churches place managers within leadership roles and as a result, they inadvertently find themselves losing momentum by heading in the wrong direction.

When they look at their systems, they think everything is fine because everything is running smoothly. But the pull to just manage the day-to-day minutia will eventually kill momentum. Your leadership team needs to be filled with leaders (agents of change) who share the common vision for where the new church is headed. Those leaders need to shape the vision that good managers can support correctly for effective, lasting change to take place. While the lead pastor will be the one who paints the vision that the Lord has brought to the church, it is their leadership team that will frame that vision so that the church as well as your managers can effectively implement it.

"Skilled leaders therefore use 'frames' to provide context and shape perspective for new proposals and plans. By framing the issues, leaders help people digest ideas in particular ways." [154] Frames should not be confused with overarching vision. The overarching vision provides a picture that your church understands as the preferred reality of where the church is headed. That vision would have come with the

---

[153] Harvard Business Review. HBR's 10 Must Reads on Change Management (Location 275). Perseus Books Group. Kindle Edition.

[154] Harvard Business Review. HBR's 10 Must Reads on Change Management (Location 416). Perseus Books Group. Kindle Edition.

resurrection of the church. "A frame can take many forms: It can be a companywide presentation that prepares employees before an unexpected change, for example, or a radio interview that provides context following an unsettling layoff." [155] The best way to frame your overarching vision is by using the pulpit.

Word pictures are often helpful to understand concepts. So, I want you to imagine that the Lord has inspired the lead pastor of a church to paint a picture. The Lord has birthed that picture into their heart, and while their expression will be unique and slightly augment the original picture, the Lord wants all to share in His vision and its beauty. The Lord has also gifted that local church and community with leaders who will help to put a frame around that picture to support it, draw attention to it and hold it in a way that others can best understand it. Our gracious God has also given effective managers to sell the art, find the best places to display it and the very best support staff to maintain it and ensure that it can be seen for generations to come. So, what does this typical structure look like in the local church?

Within the church context, elders/pastors/bishops/overseers are your vision carriers. I realize that this will look subtly different depending on your denomination or church polity. Regardless, within each church, some form of an elder/overseer exists who should own the overarching vision of the church. Remember in previous chapters that this vision came from a prayer life that allowed the Lord to share the specific form of resurrection that He was leading your church through. Now that the lead Elder has this vision, they need to communicate it from the pulpit, in the leadership gathering, and spend time sharing it with the greatest influencers of the church in every way conceivable.

As they share it, they need to be praying for discernment as to who are the leaders and managers within the church. By the way, those people are not always the ones with a title, but sometimes they are. They are not always the most vocal, but sometimes they are. When you are searching for the leaders within your church, you are looking for people who carry influence! They can gather a team and lead that

---

[155] Harvard Business Review. HBR's 10 Must Reads on Change Management (Location 416). Perseus Books Group. Kindle Edition.

team toward a preferred goal. Your conversation with the Lord on this will be paramount. Don't forget when the Lord chose His leadership team, He took a whole night to pray, and something tells me that it was not the first time that He and His Father had discussed the issue.

"¹²One of those days Jesus went out to a mountainside to pray, and spent the night praying to God. ¹³When morning came, he called his disciples to him and chose twelve of them, whom he also designated apostles". ¹⁵⁶ Every one of these apostles would lead major movements in different areas of the region upon Jesus' act of completed delegation and empowerment (Matthew 28: 16-20). They did not have a new vision, but framed Jesus' vision to share the Gospel (Good News) with the whole world! They did not have a different vision, purpose, or mission but did frame Christ's vision uniquely based on context and the diverse ethne that they were sent to reach. Additionally, they needed effective managers to accomplish Christ's mission and vision.

Your managers are typically in roles like Deacons, Directors, Ministry Leaders, community businesses and Chairmen of committees. This does not mean that managers do not have influence, but their primary gifting is the implementation and execution of the vision. Additionally, they take burdens off your most effective leaders so that those leaders can continue to hear from the Lord in prayer, preach and effectively frame the vision for the people. We also have a great Biblical example of this reality both in success and failure. Often, our greatest lessons come with failure. Acts 6: 1-7 is a great example!

> ¹ Now in these days when the disciples were increasing in number, a complaint by the Hellenists arose against the Hebrews because their widows were being neglected in the daily distribution. ² And the twelve summoned the full number of the disciples and said, "It is not right that we should give up preaching the word of God to serve tables. ³ Therefore, brothers, pick out from among you seven men of good repute, full of the Spirit and of wisdom, whom we will appoint to this duty. ⁴ But we will devote ourselves to prayer and to the ministry of the word." ⁵ And what they said pleased the

---

¹⁵⁶ *The Holy Bible: New International Version* (Lk 6:12–13). (1984). Zondervan.

whole gathering, and they chose Stephen, a man full of faith and of the Holy Spirit, and Philip, and Prochorus, and Nicanor, and Timon, and Parmenas, and Nicolaus, a proselyte of Antioch. **6** These they set before the apostles, and they prayed and laid their hands on them.

**7** And the word of God continued to increase, and the number of the disciples multiplied greatly in Jerusalem, and a great many of the priests became obedient to the faith. [157]

Notice that the leaders in this situation were trying to effectively frame Jesus' vision for the early church, but that they ran into a major management issue. This was not a small matter! Some read this passage as the Apostles were inconvenienced by the issue that widows were being overlooked in the outreach program to ensure they were being fed. That would be a misreading of what was happening in the life of the church at that moment. This was a critical issue! The Gospel would not be heard by a people group that thought they were being treated unfairly.

It was the Spirit of God that directed the Apostles to a solution that was filled with leadership wisdom. What they communicated was that they needed to stay in their lane as leaders, but that the Lord had provided the necessary managers with gifting to manage the current situation. We need to heed this Biblical paradigm and ensure that we have the right leaders and the right managers at the right place within our church. Once you have begun to identify the right leaders and managers for your change process you need to implement an effective campaign to roll out those changes to the church!

Leadership research bares out "that for change to stick, leaders must design and run an effective persuasion campaign—one that begins weeks or months before the actual turnaround plan is set in concrete." [158] Your leaders need to construct a campaign that persuades the church "that radical changes are required if it is to

---

[157] *The Holy Bible: English Standard Version* (Ac 6:1–7). (2016). Crossway Bibles.

[158] Harvard Business Review. HBR's 10 Must Reads on Change Management (Location 284). Perseus Books Group. Kindle Edition.

survive and thrive." [159] One of the reasons that you will need a different team in this season, and possibly a different seasoned leader, is that "Turnaround leaders must also gain trust by demonstrating through word and deed that they are the right leaders for the job and must convince employees that theirs is the correct plan for moving forward." [160] That is hard to do if you are seen as a part of the old leadership system. A New Team communicates a new direction; in other words, new wine that is going into new wineskins.

While prayer is the paramount and guiding force for picking the right team, there are also some tangibles that will help you in finding the right people. If you are struggling to find the right team to lead your change campaign, I would suggest reading John Maxwell's *The 21 Irrefutable Laws of Leadership*, more specifically the chapter on the *Inner Circle*.

> As you consider whether individuals should be in your inner circle, ask yourself the following questions. If you can answer yes to these questions, then they are excellent candidates for your inner circle:
>
> 1.   Do they have high influence with others?
>
> 2.   Do they bring a complementary gift to the table?
>
> 3.   Do they hold a strategic position in the organization?
>
> 4.   Do they add value to me and to the organization?
>
> 5.   Do they positively impact other inner circle members? [161]

Once you have read through Maxwell's advice, and prayed about each person, invite them to be a part of your leadership team to frame the new vision through a church

---

[159] Harvard Business Review. HBR's 10 Must Reads on Change Management (Location 293). Perseus Books Group. Kindle Edition.

[160] Harvard Business Review. HBR's 10 Must Reads on Change Management (Location 293). Perseus Books Group. Kindle Edition.

[161] Maxwell, John C. The 21 Irrefutable Laws of Leadership: Follow Them and People Will Follow You (p. 131). Kindle Edition.

campaign. Set a regular weekly meeting time with them to design the campaign. Below is what Beth Israel Deaconess Medical Center led for their "four-stage persuasion campaign:

> 1) Prepare your organization's cultural "soil" months before setting your turnaround plan in concrete— by convincing employees that your company can survive only through radical change. 2) Present your plan— explaining in detail its purpose and expected impact. 3) After executing the plan, manage employees' emotions by acknowledging the pain of change— while keeping people focused on the hard work ahead. 4) As the turnaround starts generating results, reinforce desired behavioral changes to prevent backsliding. [162]

When I began leading our change campaign at our church in 2015, I adapted and simplified the 4-step plan for the church in this way:

1. Prepare the soil

2. Present the plan

3. Execute the plan

4. Celebrate the wins

## PREPARE THE SOIL

In this phase your team's responsibility is to create a sense of urgency that radical change is necessary. After the resurrection of Christ, the church embraced an urgency to share the Gospel with the World. Connected to this urgency was the hope that they could accelerate the return of Christ. In preparing the soil your team needs to theme a campaign that highlights shared values that can be caught and embraced by the whole church. They also need to understand clearly that the church will not be returning to the way things used to be done. That the only way forward is to embrace the new vision.

---

[162] Harvard Business Review. HBR's 10 Must Reads on Change Management (Location 311). Perseus Books Group. Kindle Edition.

One of your roles as the lead pastor/elder is to ensure that your team fully understands the new vision and that they are on board. Remember to pay attention to how influence flows within the church. When I arrived at my current church, a man names Bucky Owens was the most influential member. Bucky was a Colonel in the Air Force and served as the Chair of the Finance Team. Whether I was in a leadership or church wide business meeting the current church looked to Bucky for affirmation regarding the church's direction. Bucky had also stuck it out at the church when times were hard, and the church had declined.

I knew early on that he and I needed to have a good relationship. Bucky and I had several meals and cups of coffee about the new vision of the church. He not only embraced the vision of the church, but he continued to be a vocal proponent for the power of prayer within the church. I'll never forget one of our early meetings at a local restaurant for lunch where Bucky was working to embrace the vision and he shared with me his greatest concern.

He said that with his age he may not live to see it come to fruition. At the time of the writing of this book, he is still with us, he has seen our church re-birthed and I'm hoping that he will be able to see other churches revitalized and planted with the time that he has left on this earth. He is a close friend, mentor, and confidant. He is steady and keeps me running smoothly as I plow ahead with the mission. He has helped to reshape the vision of the church many times as he helped me to frame it in the best ways possible for our church. You need leaders like him on your team.

Leaders who help you need to hone and ensure that the new vision is clear, Biblical, and simple. Continue to maintain prayer with your team as the most central thing you do both in the meeting and outside of it. Use prayer as the greatest ingredient to enrich the soil of your leadership meetings and your church meetings. Don't hesitate to add new leaders to the team if your leadership sees that they can add value to the campaign, but try and keep your leadership team between 5-7 people. If your team grows too large, it will be hard to bring concise consensus. Once you have a clear, themed, and concise campaign to present to your church then you need to move toward presenting that plan.

## PRESENT THE PLAN

Presenting the plan will be unique for each church. Ask your team what the greatest locations and times are to impact the church with the new vision. One of those times should be Sunday Worship Services. Other times may include activities like, but not limited to, prayer meetings, Bible studies, or fellowship dinners. It is critical that you do not present the whole vision and every detail in one meeting. It will be too much for the church to digest. In our case, I built an entire sermon series around the changes our team came up with that undergirded our new team's shared vision.

For instance, our team knew that spiritual warfare would be one of the things our church would face as we presented the new vision and plan. The enemy does not want the church to experience the resurrection and he will do all that he can do to come against a revitalization effort. Therefore, I wrote a six-week series on spiritual warfare entitled *All Out War* where we walked through Ephesians 6 and taught our church to put on the full armor in preparation for how the enemy was going to come against our efforts.

For our church, Sundays and Wednesday night suppers were the best two places to present the plan. In our leadership meetings, after we settled on a particular part of the plan, we would then roll it out on Sunday and provide greater conversation with the church at Wednesday night fellowship dinners. Additionally, I prepared our leaders to be able to properly answer objections to the new plan being presented. Keep in mind that not all objections will happen in a meeting of which you are a part.

One of those leaders who got hit hard by objections, more than anyone, was John Fredricks. John was my lead deacon at the time, and the leader of an adult Sunday School Class named The Gathering Class, which had been meeting since 1960. Many attendees and members of the class had been long and faithful contributors to the church. I knew that objectors to the new vision would go to trusted leaders rather than me. John was also on our leadership team helping to frame the changes of our new vision.

At almost every step of change, John received negative pushback from the more established and comfortable members of our church. He was able to answer objections based on how each phase of change was being framed and help people to receive that change or, at a minimum, quell their greatest concerns. John leveraged his leadership over our Deacons and Sunday school to frame the change that God was bringing us. I am grateful for John's leadership and influence with many of the more established and older saints of our church. I have prayed for him often, knowing that he takes more of the brunt of objections to change within our church. He is a leader that is a great defender of me as the pastor and without him, I would have given up on bringing change to our church.

Ensure that each of your leaders is framing the new vision based on their times of gathering. Also, when you gather as a church, let other leaders answer objections to the changes you are proposing so that you are not seen as the only agent of change. People are more likely to receive the proposed plan for change if they see a united front with the leadership team. Make sure you have consensus within your leadership team and that the vision has been framed in an understandable way before you move to the next step. Give your congregation plenty of moments to give feedback and create a feedback loop.

When your leaders bring back certain objections, take time in your leadership meeting to debrief and discuss those objections. One of two things will happen when you take time to talk about objections that come back to you through the feedback loop. First, you will be able to use collective wisdom to best understand the congregations' concerns and develop a shared response. Because you developed the response as a team, you will have equipped not only the leader who brought the objection but the whole team to respond. If one leader brought up the objection, you can be certain that others in the congregation are thinking about it. Now your whole team knows how to respond in a unified way.

The second option is that the objection provided may be a legitimate concern. When you discuss this with your team, they may give legitimacy to the objection. Then, you can work with the team to adjust the change plan. While this second reality is more humbling, it is also more powerful. The congregation will know that they have been heard and that you spent time in prayer and discussion regarding their objection. You will gain respect with that kind of humility and your congregation and team will learn that you are willing to adjust the plan when legitimate concerns are brought up. Talk about winning friends and influencing people! [163]

Throughout this whole phase communicate the vision in every way you and your team can. Vision comes easily to visionaries, but not to the rest of the world. They need to hear it over and over again. Bill Hybels is credited with saying that "Vision Leaks," and on this point, he was right. When you are tired of sharing the vision and you feel like you have communicated it ad nauseam, then you are ready to execute. But even after you execute, continue to remind people about the vision. The people, just like Israel in the desert, need a constant reminder of what the goal or prize is.

## EXECUTE THE PLAN

At this phase, you need to gather your managers and structure their interface with your leadership. This is my weakest area! My personality and gifting are grounded in vision. It is rare to find a visionary who can effectively execute the details of the plan. If you are a visionary, have the humility to admit this and even if you are the rare unicorn in this regard, remember that it takes a team to lead and execute a major change process.

Your managers will be the ones helping your leaders to best know how to resource and implement the plan within various contexts across your church. To effectively equip them, carefully break the vision down into specific goals and objectives. Goals are specific outcomes that will support the vision that your leadership will own. Objectives are specific measurable steps that will support specified goals and your management team owns these.

Equip your leaders with the right goals, and then coach them to lead your management teams to create the right supporting objectives. Make certain you continue to meet with your leadership team often and allow them to give updates from your management teams based on specific goals and objectives. Ensure that each management team knows that they are heard and that their leaders represent them well at the leadership meeting. Be willing to adjust where you need to. Don't

---

[163] Carnegie, Dale (1936). How To Win Friends and Influence People. New York: Simon and Schuster

get hung up on the size of your team. If your team is small then take on just a few goals and objectives at a time.

In addition, keep a close eye on the mood of the church as change is executed. It is not uncommon for people to get frustrated and discouraged. Change is hard and as you sense the mood shifting to a negative realm, work with your team to address the mood. Don't shy away from taking a small break to just celebrate and spend time together without having to work on the vision. Make sure you ask often how people are doing with the changes and how your team is addressing people's moods.

If you are having a hard time figuring out where to start with goals and objectives, look for low-hanging fruit. When looking, just ask your team to fill in the following blank: "Everyone has known for a long time that _____ needs to change but no one has had the guts to address it." When you answer this question, you find what I like to call a momentum multiplier. Because there is a large consensus on this issue, bringing healthy change to it through your team will multiply momentum for change and increase the church's confidence in your team's ability to lead healthy change.

Early on at Grace Seaford Church, I realized that there was no healthy children's ministry. We had a few faithful folks who were keeping the children's church alive, but the idea of having dedicated resources for children and visiting families was almost nonexistent. This was a glaring issue, and the church leadership knew it. The goal: Create a healthy children's ministry for families from birth to fifth grade. At this phase of the church, I had a small pool to draw from, but I had some good leaders and managers to assist in this change process.

Once I assembled our team and brought up the issue and how it was connected to our vision to reach families with the Gospel, they affirmed that this was a long-standing problem. My leaders helped me to frame the issue for the church family. My wife and I completely cleaned and prepared the old nursery. A few of the older ladies of our church came by and asked us why we were cleaning the nursery since we did not have any children. My wife said that by faith, we are preparing for what God is about to do. This was my wife leading by framing faith around the vision to reach families with the Gospel.

We began to increase our footprint on social media to create an image that Grace was creating a healthy space for families. I worked with my Associate Pastor (Bud Rager) to create a children's message as a part of our adult service and my wife began to assist the faithful few leaders to create a healthy children's program. The children's program was brought up and framed as a priority in the Deacon's meeting, in leadership meetings, and in the business meetings of the church. As an aside, Pastor Bud Rager moved to South Carolina and continues to work on revitalizing churches. I love it when God sends leaders out to expand His Kingdom!

My finance chair (Bucky Owens) and I talked about the need to staff the program if it were to be successful. Leaders were praying now for the right person. Bucky knew that the budget could not work for my role, an associate pastor (part time) and a children's minister. So, I started at the church intentionally bi-vocational. These were all critical management aspects that needed to be addressed if we were to achieve our goal. We brought on a part-time Children's Director, and in working with her, we shaped the vision more clearly. The vision was shaped into a child having such a good time learning about Jesus that they begged their parents to come back to church.

Our trustees (management) had to create greater space for the children's program and invest financial resources into its renovation: critical aspects of undergirding the vision. Each of these management issues were objectives that were created and benchmarked so that we could achieve our goal. Our children's ministry started growing and we would ask children who came what they thought of the church. They responded that they loved it, and could not wait to come back!

This process was repeated with student ministry, recovery ministry and worship ministry. Goals and objectives were framed based on the vision of the church to reach families in our community with the Gospel of Christ. It took receiving a vision from God, adding good leaders, and supporting those leaders with gifted managers who equipped and resourced that vision. Because this phase requires so much work and investment, people will want to know that it has been worth it. That is why you must celebrate each successful step!

## CELEBRATE THE WINS

You better believe that we celebrated every win in our children's program: every new family, baptism, and new children's leader! We talked about it in our leadership meetings, from the pulpit, deacon's meetings, and in staff meetings. Momentum was building and the church was growing. In that first year, there were more baptisms than in many years in the past. Celebrating your wins changes your church's perspective and mood. In this season we created our values: Gather, Grow, Give, and Go.

We began to celebrate wins over each of these values as we implemented change after change. Pretty soon change was the norm! Older saints were excited to see the halls filled with children again and baptisms taking place, and because sharing wins all the time was happening across our strata, they shared those wins with everyone in their circle of influence. It was changing the mood of the church!

Make sure that you celebrate the wins in the context of your values and vision. This reinforces and multiplies momentum headed in the right direction. Don't think there will not be naysayers to the change you are bringing. But when your team, managers and the bulk of your church is alive and sharing the wins, it will extinguish the negative comments like water to a fire. I have found that sharing the wins must be more than a program or change process; it has to be woven into your very DNA.

Like most churches, Grace has small groups. We call them Growth Groups. When we were launching groups, we had to determine what would constitute a group. This took some thought and prayer. We had diverse people of age, backgrounds, and church experience. I was in prayer one day, in year two of our revitalization, when it dawned on me that there were three qualities that every successful group I had been in shared. I have been in Sunday Schools, Men's Bible Studies, Couples Small Groups, and Community Bible Studies. In every successful group, they centered on God's Word, they prayed for one another, and they shared their living testimony often.

I distilled this down into the WWW (Word, Win, Wrestle). We asked our people to gather in a small group with people that they wanted to share their lives with and share the WWW. They pick the context for their gathering: couples in a home, Sunday school, morning coffee, or basketball on the weekend. They would share a word from their devotion or pick a book of the Bible to study (WORD). They would share one way that week that they saw God at work in their life (WIN). They would share one way that they were struggling personally and pray as a group over that struggle (WRESTLE).

What is most interesting is that I discovered our groups struggled the most with the WINS! With the pressures and negative world we live in, people had a hard time envisioning how God was at work. But because they were part of a weekly group that shared WINS, they began to look more for God's hand. I also learned what happens within your groups impacts the culture of your church. Before I knew it Word, Win, Wrestle became a part of staff meetings, planning sessions, deacons, ministries, and missions. And where we celebrated how God was at work the people's mood was lifted and encouraged.

Celebrate the WINS within your change process at every level of your church! You will be amazed at how people sharing their testimony of how the living God is alive among them will change their perspective and amplify momentum. After all, we are reminded in Revelation that the saints overcame Satan "by the blood of the Lamb and by the word of their testimony"[164] Never underestimate the power of a testimony.

## RINSE AND REPEAT

This change process will be repeated as you create a healthy church. Guard against the idea that "we have finally arrived"; therefore, are now safe from ever dying again. Instead, remind the church and your leadership often that DEATH, BURIAL, and RESURRECTION are normal aspects of the crucified life. Remind them *"[22] to put off your old self, which belongs to your former manner of life and is corrupt through deceitful desires, [23] and to be renewed in the spirit of your minds, [24] and to put on the new self, created after the likeness of God in true righteousness and holiness." [165]*

---

[164] *The Holy Bible: English Standard Version* (Re 12:10–11). (2016). Crossway Bibles.

[165] *The Holy Bible: English Standard Version* (Eph 4:22–24). (2016). Crossway Bibles.

Indeed, preach the crucified life and continue to call the church to faithful obedience as the Lord leads you into new adventures. In each new adventure, you will need to die again to yourself and to what you thought should happen so that the Lord can create something new. Don't forget Paul's warning to the church in Galatia:

> O foolish Galatians! Who has bewitched you? It was before your eyes that Jesus Christ was publicly portrayed as crucified. ² Let me ask you only this: Did you receive the Spirit by works of the law or by hearing with faith? ³ Are you so foolish? Having begun by the Spirit, are you now being perfected by the flesh? [166]

My church, even now, is going through another death. We are having to restructure our leadership to support the Lord's expanding vision. We are sensing that our Lord is calling our church to take on a greater role in church planting and sending leaders to parts of our area where the Gospel is not being proclaimed. This will require another DEATH, BURIAL and RESURRECTION. But it will be worth it to see God continue to move in our fellowship and in our church. There are current leaders and attenders who struggle with this new change. But the change process is being repeated and we are seeing the faithfulness of Jesus as we move forward into a crucified life that brings resurrection.

I pray that your church and leadership might embrace the crucified life, that you will hear our Lord's voice clearly as he calls you to follow him. I am certain that He will provide a unique pathway forward for your church. Do "not grow weary of doing good, for in due season we will reap, if we do not give up." [167] May you experience the miracle that only God can bring, have the compassion to lead your church through its grief process, the humility to accept what the Lord brings as His intended resurrection for your gathering and finally the leadership to lead your church, so that it might fully embrace all that God has purposed and planned for them!

---

[166] *The Holy Bible: English Standard Version* (Ga 3:1–3). (2016). Crossway Bibles.

[167] *The Holy Bible: English Standard Version* (Ga 6:9). (2016). Crossway Bibles.

## NEXT STEPS

1. Search your team and church for anyone who has experience with leading a change process or understands Change Management. You may want to put out a bulletin announcement or Facebook post.

2. Reach out to consultants, business leaders, and denominational representatives and see if they have experience with Change Management.

3. Purchase *HBR's 10 Must Reads on Change Management (including featured article "Leading Change," by John P. Kotter)*. Begin to acquaint yourself with the change process and successful models of leading change.

4. With your leadership decide which Change Management model you will use.

5. Pick one area or issue to use the change process over and follow through. Celebrate how that change brings you a step closer to the vision you have painted. Note: pick an area that most people within the church know needs to change and will give you the biggest bang for your buck.

6. Repeat for each area of change that you and your team have identified.

# Conclusion

*"God opposes the proud but gives grace to the humble."*[168]

*Follow the money and you will know why things work the way they work – Dottie Davis*
*(My Mom)*

At my core, I am a prideful man. I knew this early on in my Christian journey and that is why I grabbed ahold of James 4:6. As I write the conclusion to this book, I am still in search of the right publishing partner. I have several contracts before me, but I am concerned that my pride could rise to destroy or diminish this work. It would be easy to pick the one who could best get my work out there. But at the end of the day, it really is not *my work*: it is Christ's. Not that it is infallible like our Savior, not that I feel capable of speaking for our King, but my Savior prodded me to write what I have written. I believe that the Lord called me to write this book because He wanted His church to be awakened to DEATH, BURIAL, and RESURRECTION!

Additionally, my mother always told me to "follow the money". She saw a world of greed around her, and over her lifetime, she was able to follow the trajectory of greed to discover human purpose. When I was a younger man, I thought my mom was wrong about this because she was jaded by so many hurts in this life. But the older I have become, the more I have seen her wisdom. People take advantage of another's desire to grow in their faith and the church's desire to grow as a congregation. Books and studies are written to capitalize on this very issue. I do not want this work to be one more that does the same.

---

[168] *The Holy Bible: New International Version* (Jas 4:6). (1984). Zondervan.

Therefore, I am praying for the right partners to publish and distribute this book. I am praying for the right networks to share its wisdom, not for profit, but for God's glory as He awakens His church to His mission. I want to die to what *I* want, so that Christ might raise His wisdom shared within this work to bless His Bride (The Church). As you read this conclusion, I humbly ask you to pray that God will keep me humble, that He will use this work for His glory, and that church leaders will share it, and build upon it.

As you make decisions about where to lead your church, ensure that you are practicing humility. Ensure that money is not your motivating factor. Pray that we all would *empty* (Kenosis) ourselves of what we think is owed to us and would instead live out a crucified life (Philippians 2). I am praying for you and your church. I am praying that you experience a glorious death to who you were so that you can experience a miraculous resurrection as Christ calls you to a new life in Him. I am praying that your church's resurrection will impact many in the community around you and that many sons and daughters come to know Jesus as a result!

Our Savior is knocking at the door (Rev. 3:20) and He is hopeful that you and your church will open it. May our God bless you and admonish you with a crucified life, and may you have the humility to receive it. As we conclude our time together, please receive a benediction from Paul's letter to Rome: "May the God of hope fill you with all joy and peace in believing, so that by the power of the Holy Spirit you may abound in hope." [169]

AMEN!

---

[169] *The Holy Bible: English Standard Version* (Ro 15:13). (2016). Crossway Bibles.

# Bibliography

Al, I.-I. (1999). Culture and Psychopathology. In D. G. Benner & P. C. Hill (Eds.), *Baker encyclopedia of psychology & counseling* (2nd ed.). Baker Books.

Carnegie, Dale (1936). How To Win Friends and Influence People. New York: Simon and Schuster

Harvard Business Review. HBR's 10 Must Reads on Change Management (including featured article 'Leading Change,' by John P. Kotter). Perseus Books Group. Kindle Edition.

Blackaby, H., & Blackaby, R. (2001). *Spiritual Leadership: Moving People on to God's Agenda*. B&H Publishing Group.

Clifton, Mark. Reclaiming Glory: Creating a Gospel Legacy throughout North America. B&H Publishing Group. Kindle Edition.

Clinton, T., & Hawkins, R. (2009). *The Quick-Reference Guide to Biblical Counseling: Personal and Emotional Issues*. Baker Books.

Green, Michael. Evangelism in the Early Church. Kindle Edition.

Darabont, Frank (Director). 1995. *The Shawshank Redemption*. Warner Bros. Entertainment Inc.

Kniskern, J. W. (1993). *When the vow breaks: a survival and recovery guide for Christians facing divorce*. Broadman & Holman Publishers.

Knowles, A. (2001). *The Bible guide* (1st Augsburg books ed., p. 144). Augsburg.

Kübler-Ross, Elisabeth. On Death and Dying: What the Dying Have to Teach Doctors, Nurses, Clergy and Their Own Families. Scribner. Kindle Edition.

Kübler-Ross, Elisabeth; Kessler, David. On Grief and Grieving: Finding the Meaning of Grief Through the Five Stages of Loss. Scribner. Kindle Edition.

Lewis, C. S.. Mere Christianity (C.S. Lewis Signature Classics). HarperCollins. Kindle Edition.

Lucado, M. (1987). *God came near: chronicles of the Christ*. Multnomah Press.

Lucado, M. (1996). *Life lessons from the inspired word of God: book of Romans*. Word Pub.

Maxwell, John C. The 21 Irrefutable Laws of Leadership: Follow Them and People Will Follow You. Kindle Edition.

Mullins, E. Y. (1908). *The Axioms of Religion: A New Interpretation of the Baptist Faith*. The Griffith & Rowland Press.

Northouse, Peter G.. Leadership: Theory and Practice. SAGE Publications. Kindle Edition.

O'Dell, Shannon. Transforming Church in Rural America. Master Books. Kindle Edition.

Peterson, Eugene H.. The Pastor: A Memoir. HarperCollins. Kindle Edition.

Rainer, Thom S.. Autopsy of a Deceased Church: 12 Ways to Keep Yours Alive. B&H Publishing Group. Kindle Edition.

Rogers, E. M. (1962). *Diffusion of Innovations* (1st ed.). Collier-Macmillan, Ltd.

Rutledge, Fleming. The Crucifixion: Understanding the Death of Jesus Christ. Wm. B. Eerdmans Publishing Co. Kindle Edition.

Ryrie, C. C. (1999). *Basic Theology: A Popular Systematic Guide to Understanding Biblical Truth* (pp. 48–49). Moody Press.

Scullard, Mark; Wilhelm, Emma; Sugerman, Jeffrey. The 8 Dimensions of Leadership: DiSC Strategies for Becoming a Better Leader. Berrett-Koehler Publishers. Kindle Edition.

Shelley, M. (1986). *Helping those who don't want help*. Christianity Today, Inc.; Word Books.

*Statistics and Reasons for Church Decline*. (n.d.). Statistics and Reasons for Church Decline. Retrieved January 21, 2022, from http://www.churchleadership.org/apps/articles/default.asp?articleid=42346

Stobierski, T. (2020, January 21). ORGANIZATIONAL CHANGE MANAGEMENT: WHAT IT IS & WHY IT'S IMPORTANT. Harvard Business School Online. https://online.hbs.edu/blog/post/organizational-change-management.

*The Holy Bible: English Standard Version*. (2016). Crossway Bibles.

*The Holy Bible: New International Version* (Lk 6:12–13). (1984). Zondervan.

Tolstoy, L. (1886). *The Death of Ivan Ilych*. United States: Seven Treasure Publications.

Warren, Rick. The Purpose Driven Life: What on Earth Am I Here For?. Zondervan. Kindle Edition.

---

*Pastor Larry Davis*

Larry Davis is available for author interviews. For more information contact:

Larry Davis
Advantage Books
info@advbooks.com

To purchase additional copies of this book or any other book that we publish, visit our bookstore at www.advbookstore.com

Orlando, Florida, USA
*"we bring dreams to life"*™
www.advbookstore.com

Printed in the USA
CPSIA information can be obtained
at www.ICGtesting.com
LVHW020713010224
770552LV00003B/11

9 781597 557818